UBER – Good or Bad Economy

10 Insights Into the
Biggest Disruption of Our Era

Kevin Lý

UBER – *Good Or Bad Economy*
Book link: *www.BookonUBER.com* or *www.fb.com/UberBook.KevinLy*

Copyright © 2016, KEVIN LÝ

Publisher
10-10-10 Publishing
Markham, ON
Canada
Printed in the United States of America

ISBN 978-1-77277-102-2

Contents

Praise for the Author

"I trust Kevin Lý's competency in international business relation and branding expertise. You will see this as you read thoroughly through his economics books. *UBER – Good Or Bad Economy* is a great book for entrepreneurs and politicians".

Davis Thach
President and CEO at TD Global Enterprise™

Dedication

To Momoka Kubo, Angela Himari, and the Lý family

Acknowledgements

I am grateful to Mr. Davis Thach, the President & CEO of CDC Corporation/TD Global Enterprise, Mr. Carlos Nieves (Vice President, Corporation & Business), Mr. Paul Leary (Ph.D & Vice President, Business Analysts), Mr. Bruce Johnson (Civil Engineering & Project Manager), and Mr. Jim Gilmore (Architecture Engineering of TD Global Enterprise). These are among the most successful entrepreneurs in The United States of America. Successive business plans of CDC Corporation – TD Global Enterprise are multi-million dollar projects for multi-billion super-profitable investments, especially luxurious condominiums and skyscrapers projects in Boston, Massachusetts, U.S.A. It is my honor to have meetings with Mr. Davis Thach (President & CEO of TD Global Enterprise) in person. His broad vision and professional formula for success has helped to shape my business disciplines and strategies for my achievements.

I am also dedicating my book as a result from meeting with Sharon Lechter, the co-author of Rich Dad Poor Dad (by Robert T Kiyosaki) in a business conference in 2016 in Toronto, Canada. Sharon is such a nice woman with a gentle voice in real life, but she has a unique and effective way of showing the key successful business tactics to me through a simple and friendly talk.

It's also my honor to know Mr. Shaun McKenna, former Sales & Merchandising President at Mosaic CANADA, former Sales & Marketing President, and now Executive VP (Strategic Channels) at Acosta. Meeting with Shaun in the earlier years helped to build a strong foundation for my present and future success in the business world.

Foreword

This book will take you on an incredible learning journey and will deepen your understanding with UBER services. It is a true pleasure to write Kevin Lý's foreword for his book, *UBER – Good Or Bad Economy*. Technology is so fascinating to me. You live in an era where technology is fast evolving, most notably into industries, where in the past, technology was not the primary platform. For example, companies like, UBER, AirBnB, Tinder, Facebook, computerized apps, Tesla and Google's Self-driving research and more. I have never before felt more delighted to engage with technology and innovation until I read Kevin's book, *UBER - Good Or Bad Economy.*

Kevin's economic analysis and discussion in this book is an incredible tour guide that will take you through the stages of rideshare innovation. Kevin explains all of the business procedures to you and clears up any confusion that you may have about UBER. He shows you the real value and importance of UBER services and how it will affect you. *UBER - Good or Bad Economy* is Kevin's work of art. Learn from Kevin as he enriches your knowledge and empowers your worldwide view.

Raymond Aaron
New York Times Bestselling Author

Notice to Readers

Dear Readers,

Thank you for your support and appreciation in regards to my time and effort to accomplish this book. This book is merely to discuss numerous business insights to show how important technology is. The useful sources of information and opinion within this book are personal expressions and feedbacks gathered from UBER Partner Networks or forums that I have managed or followed (Go here: fb.com/groups/UberToronto). This is not legal advice. It is your government's responsibility and decision to accommodate rideshare or other services in your city. I have done my best to make the following content fair, helpful, and correct.

Please contact me: www.fb.com/KevinLy.Official for any suggestions, questions, or corrections.

About this Book

Through useful sources and feedback, we believe that we can bring the most valuable service to our city in terms of employment protection, consumer satisfaction, business and economy growth, as well as public health & safety.

Chapter 1: UBER SYSTEMS

1.1 CEO and Co-founder's story to start Uber:

In 2008, on a snowy Paris evening, Travis Kalanick, CEO of Uber, and his co-founder, Garrett Camp, tried to order a taxi, but all the cabs were taken. What they saw on the streets were all private cars. They would have loved to pay any driver of one of these cars to pick them up and give them a ride. They found that this was inconvenient. After their business trip, they came up with a business idea that allows a rider to share the ride in a private car by requesting this through an app on a smartphone. At a busy time, like national holidays, it is difficult to catch a cab. So, why do the number of vehicles on the road far outnumber the number of cabs? They thought about creating a business by using the private cars on the road. It would actually help the environment.

That is when the great idea of ridesharing, UberCab (the first time name), was born! Travis Kalanick has an engineering background. He also hired an experienced, Vietnamese-American, senior engineer to join his team. They first worked on the app, and then started out by having four cars on the San Francisco streets. With a great marketing strategy (promotion code), the business became a phenomenon since it brings real value to the people in the city. Now, Uber is one of the largest multi-billion valuation companies in more than 66 countries and 507 cities around the world (as of August 2016).

1.2 A complicated mobile application:

People can see that Uber is a simple mobile application. However, it is a perfect combination of tech complex. Uber APP partners with more than 20 third party libraries. It needs a GPS connection system (Google Maps, Waze, Uber traffic map) and works with a payment transaction through the other app (Braintree, CardIO, eBay). It needs an app for password security (1PasswordExtention), face ID creation and restore, Uber ride trip calling notifications, surge pricing application, Uber partner feedback and appraisal form, light and sound notification system, and traffic and events notification system.

1.3 Uber platforms:

UberX is the most popular Uber platform whenever we mention Uber. UberX is the most economic of private cars. As a part of Toronto's new regulation, UberX vehicles must not be more than seven years old. The only, and most accurate, way to recognize your Uber car is to look at the plate number, since every car has a unique number on it. Other information you can use to identify when your Uber is coming is: make, color, and model, and the driver's face.

There is a difference between the UberX private driver and the original private driver that a businessman hires: The one whom a rich man hires to drive for him is a salary worker and obeys whatever his boss commands. He may be treated badly sometimes depending on his boss's mood. However, an UberX driver is anyone who passes the requirement and background check with his qualified vehicle. He/ she may be a general worker who drives as a secondary job. He/she may be a college student. He/she may be a professional who has a desk job in the daytime. He/she may be a teacher who drives on his/her free time. He/she may be a startup owner who needs some cash for a little investment. He/she may be a grandparent who is retired. Those who drive for Uber are their own boss (Are you really your own boss? Read through to find out the answer!). If you, as a passenger, are in a bad mood or displaying unintentional behavior, you are treating your UberX driver as a "traditional" private driver. The chances are that you may be kicked out of his/her vehicle in the middle of your route. Uber has learned and tried to create a fairly good experience for both riders and driver partners.

As we can see from the app, Uber also has other high-class and multi-purposed platforms such as *UberBlack, UberSelect, UberAccess (UberAssist + UberWAV), UberTaxi, UberHop, UberPool,* and *UberBike* – it varies in each city depending on demand and economy. There is an XL size for all these platforms. UberBlack and UberSelect vehicles, which are authorized to operate in most airports, are better than UberX. UberBlack (black inside and out, leather) is the fancy Uber platform for high-class people or for important gigs (See the list: BookonUber.com). UberHop is for the city commuters. At a given time and at the same pickup zone, three individuals who live in the same area are picked up by the same Uber driver. UberHop is the most economic platform. It is a real carpool with a flat fare. The driver gets paid a little more and the riders pay less. UberHop has a specific schedule on the day (business hours). UberPool is a similar great idea. UberPool doesn't pick up at the same time; it just goes in the same directions. UberPool is 30% cheaper than UberX – sometimes matched, sometimes not. In this matter, UberPool drivers earn less than expected. With UberAccess, there are two forms: UberAssist and UberWAV. UberAssist is for first time riders, and ensures that they have a good first experience with Uber.   It also avoids crazy surge pricing for the first trips. Uber shares their commission percentage with UberAssist drivers. UberWAV is for disabled passengers. UberTaxi works with local taxis to add cars to their fleets. This platform was applied for the earlier stage of developing Uber. UberTaxi is confusing and not very popular. These drivers are the only drivers that get a tip percentage added in with the fare. With different economy and traffic in some Asian countries, there is the helpful UberBike (motor bike and bicycle) to beat the traffic in rush hour. UberX is the most popular platform. Sometimes when in high demand, you will see, "UberX is not available." But that doesn't mean all UberX have been taken. Uber tries to shorten the pickup time. This time, Uber intentionally wants you to try other Uber platforms. Most people seem to order UberX.

Even businessmen or rich people order UberX. Other Uber platform drivers usually have to wait a long time for a ride. That is the reason Uber enabled those Uber vehicles to pick up UberX passengers! Uber partners of these vehicles are not happy with that. With their expensive cars, they aren't supposed to earn at an UberX rate.

1.4 Surge pricing:

What is surge pricing? This is the most interesting and sensitive topic when people talk about Uber. Surge pricing happens when the demand over the supply of the service rate at a location suddenly turns higher and higher. In order to meet the demand, Uber has to attract and bring more and more drivers from other areas, or go offline to the busy location, or back to online.

The riders who are new to the Uber platforms, or those who are from low-income families don't like the idea. Some even hate surge pricing.

Why does Uber have surge pricing? Uber receives hundreds of surge complaints per day, but why doesn't Uber ever remove it from the business? It has been this way for years. Just imagine that removing surge pricing from the Uber system would be like trying to remove the beating heart from a living human body, or like removing the battery out of your smart-phone. Surge pricing is really important for Uber. It is the most incredible job attraction to bring professionals, who are willing to quit their desk jobs, on board to drive for Uber. Driver partners find it motivating and worth driving, just like when ants find their sweet piece of food.

Surge pricing also helps to keep the actual taxi business. When the surge is more than twice the price, some riders who are from low-income families can't afford to choose to give up on Uber, but they will take a taxi as an alternative means of transport at that moment. That explains why the cabs are still around, although the Uber fare is much cheaper.

How powerful is the surge pricing?
Many Uber drivers own expensive cars. They don't want dogs, cats, or smelly food in their cars, so they will refuse trips for those reasons. They usually use the excuse that they accept service dogs only, or the excuse that they are worried about the next riders who may be allergic to animal fur. However, with a high surge, they are willing to accept these, no matter how stinky the animal or food is. With surge pricing, they even accept the rides for small children, without car seat! A driver would skip their appointment or family gathering, or even New Year Eve, and would come from far away to pick you up for a ride, if the surge is doubled or tripled! Surging is something that motivates them to wake up early in the morning. That is why Uber is available at all times. Surge pricing boosts Uber revenue magically through statutory holidays, sporting events, bad weather, etc. People hate bad weather, but Uber drivers don't. They love tornadoes, hurricanes, floods,

tsunamis, heavy rains, snowstorms, and thunderstorms. They love public transit down time, and all other occasions that lead to a crazy surge. This means that drivers earn much more.

Surging is different depending on the city and the economy. If you see surge pricing often, that is a good sign for your city's economy because it only happens in strong and healthy economy zones. We hardly ever find surge pricing in rural areas. Many customers don't understand the surge very well. They usually ask why the surge is turned on in their area when there are available cars nearby around the corners. The answer is that the surge rate is based on the overall demand at the radius of the broader location. If the *riders to drivers* online ratio is 100%-80%, the surge is 2.0X. If the *riders to drivers* online ratio is 100%-70%, the surge is 3.0X. Or, on statutory holidays like Christmas or New Years Eve, the riders demand surges more than 5.0X (with *riders to drivers* online ratio being more than 100%-50%), and so on.

Important note: We need to comprehend the *riders to drivers* online rate. The rider is considered to be online as soon as the Uber application is opened and they are about to request a ride. However, the times that the drivers are being counted as being online are when they turn their GPS on! That's why some drivers who chase the high rate (surge), wonder why the surge is off as they stay offline. They forget that their GPSs are on! Uber uses a location connection (GPS) to know exactly where their drivers are! Some top earning drivers doubtfully feel that Uber even knows they are online when they use the rider app. There is no evidence for it, but Uber is smarter since they are a technology company with a top senior engineering team.

Another question about surge pricing is why a number of people still keep taking Uber while the surge is extremely high. The answer is different here: They are rich. They are in a rush. They are Uber fans and are loyal to Uber. They are willing to pay a little more to avoid "dirty" cabs. They don't plan to take an Uber ahead of time. They prefer to ride in a private car. They feel fancier this way. They like most Uber drivers. It is their habit. They don't care how much they spend. They believe Uber still cheaper and more affordable compared to a taxi. They pay extra to top drivers. Drunk people want to get home as quick as possible. When there is no taxi available, they have no other choice.

Math mastery is surge pricing's success story: The most extraordinary reason why surge pricing is working so well in daily commuting is that Uber wisely picked the right mathematical fraction. Uber does not use percentage! What if Uber says: "Now it is surge pricing and you have to pay 250% of the fare." Most of the riders will refuse right off the bat! Instead, Uber uses 2.5X (surge). Some riders who are terrible at math think they just need to pay a few dollars (like two loonies and fifty cents) extra! Yes, it is real. On the other hand, if you accept the *surge priced* trip, chances are that you will get one of the top, smartest drivers in the city. It is either because of their high IQ, or luck. Those riders who take surged trips are appreciated as sponsors for the new ridesharing service in the city.

Another interesting question is, "Who *creates* the surge?" Of course, it is not made up by drivers. If the surge were made by drivers, they would make it 1000 times higher in order to maximize their earnings. The surge is created by Uber engineers and calculated automatically based on demand through the Uber app. Demand depends on the number of drivers at the time. Uber authorizes the applying of the surge, but the drivers are the ones who directly control it. If a number of drivers all go offline at the same time, for a certain amount of time, the service demand will pick up, based on the online rate. However, it never happens! Not many drivers do that! Only 20% are top earning driver partners whose brains are brighter and smarter. They know what time and to which location to drive to, in order to maximize their earnings. The others have low IQs or just do Uber for fun. They are probably new driver partners. They have no idea how the system works. They are not following any social forum for drivers to learn how to earn big. They are in need of cash and want to do something for a short time. They don't have enough time to chase the surge. In chapter 5, we will discuss the question: How much do Uber drivers really earn? We will also find out about income differentiation among Uber drivers. In Toronto, we have the Uber Toronto Facebook group: facebook.com/groups/UberToronto, where drivers find help and support. The top driver partners are pro-active members of this forum.

That's also the reason why Uber has been spending a lot on advertising and promotion to attract new drivers to keep the system running smoothly and affordably. Every day, thousands of new drivers register to join the service.

1.5 How to pick up at the airport:

Up until now, more and more riders have learned the trick of ordering an UberX at the airports, where UberX operation is restricted or prohibited. People are choosing UberX to save money. When you land at the airport, you will not see an UberX option available on an app. There are mostly UberBlack or UberSelect available. In order to order an UberX, and save money, you have to move your *ping* out of the airport map zone, as near as possible, and then request. Right after you request, you call your driver to notify that you are actually in the airport terminal. Most drivers are happy to drive an extra mile to pick you up. They believe airport pickup is a long ride, so why not? The airport pickup happens every single day without much trouble because the authority officers have no idea which vehicle is an UberX. It is private. To make sure it is safe for you, the driver, point him in the direction of a spot that is less busy with traffic, and tell him to be ready at the curb. The enforcement officers are very strict, and give out tickets, which could cost your driver from $70 and up.

1.6 Uber innovation:

Uber drivers are those who experience the future map ahead of time. In fact, you will see the cars moving on GPS maps in real time in the next decade. Uber map is really helpful. It turns red if the traffic is bad. Green means that the traffic is clear. By looking and counting how heavy traffic is on a route, you are able to keep going on that street, or divert to another similar direction with less traffic.

According to Wikipedia, as of May 28, 2016, Uber service is available in over 66 countries and 449 cities all over the world. They are all different depending on the economy, culture and infrastructure. With one single app, you can order in any city where you want to go. It is that convenient. In some cities, Uber is more affordable to ride when compared to cabs. In some other cities, Uber is something that is too fancy to take as private transit. In Hanoi, people freak out when they take a *Taxi Dù* (private taxi cab under a single owner). It's just like an UberX . The difference is that you have no idea in advance how much your trip will cost you. It is usually a very expensive one. It is totally overcharged. You are asked to pay in cash. So, be aware when you come to the capital of Vietnam and try to order a *Taxi Dù*.

1.7 Why no phone service?

As a fast growing company with a multi-billion dollar valuation, a calling service is really something that challenges the company. With the business model embracing technology's periodical updates, there are a lot of misunderstood interactions or frustrating complaints sent out every single day from impatient riders and drivers. People are advised to send Uber Support an email at Support@Uber.com (for customers), and at PartnersYourCity@Uber.com (e.g.: PartnersToronto @Uber.com, for drivers). Though we, as either riders or drivers, can't find a phone number to call Uber for daily issues, Uber does have a 24/7 emergency phone number for serious reports such as accidents or safety concerns. As of August 2016, there are Uber phone services that are activated in some selected cities and states. You can check with your local office.

Chapter 2: UBER & RUMORS

2.1 Understanding licensing:

In Canada and the USA, most businesses are required to have a specific registration or license to protect consumer health and safety. Even nail salons, hair salons, massage parlors, or spas must be licensed.

In the beginning, when Uber was still not well known to the public, a lot of people were in doubt and would ask Uber drivers to show a *license* when they were going to take an Uber ride. The stereotype of licensing makes people rely on licensing or reputation in order to trust a business. That's why some people hesitate to start taking Uber until all their friends and family have tried it for a while.

As described, when Uber first started, Uber drivers were private drivers willing to share a ride. The idea of ridesharing was still new. Of course, each driver has to obtain a class G license. Uber vehicles are allowed to pick up from one to seven passengers (max). If Uber drivers had to operate a truck, a school bus, or a coach, they would have to get different licenses (D,G, A with "R", E, F) rather than G. According to The Ontario Ministry of Transportation, you can operate an ambulance with just a full G license.

In Canada, a driver license card (G) is actually considered as an official government photo ID. In Toronto, when you are 16 years of age or older, you can start applying for one at any Service Ontario office. In order to register to drive for Uber, a driver must be insured with sufficient coverage for property and personal damage. Uber also has ongoing education information in the app for drivers, so as to make sure these operators behave properly, professionally, and safely by law. In addition, in Toronto, Uber has successfully contracted with Intact Insurance Company to make sure all drivers are now covered as well. From the beginning, Uber confidently told people that all riders would be backed by five million dollars insurance in case of a severe accident. In 2016, when new rideshare regulation kicked in, Uber agreed to pay a $20,000 one-time registration fee.

In addition to the city appealing to technology and innovation, the city of Toronto granted a PTC (Private Transportation Company) license to Uber. Uber is officially legalized to operate in Toronto.

That is the *license* we speak of, not the one that is just vaguely asked for because of rumor and doubt.

In Chapter 7 (Uber legalization challenge), we will discuss more details about Uber operation licensing in Canada and other countries around the world.

2.2 Does Uber own Uber cars?

Uber is a technology company whose engineers are being hired to design and develop the ride-hailing application to connect private drivers to people who want a shared ride. The fact is, Uber, the world largest taxi company, owns no vehicles! This is the trending economic and smart business idea. Similarly, Airbnb, the world's largest accommodation provider, owns no real estate. Facebook, the world's most popular social media, creates no content. Alibaba, the most valuable retailer, has no inventory. Tinder, the world's most popular dating service, has no single individual to offer. People and businesses are throwing billions and billions of dollars into these service platforms on a day-to-day basis.

The *Uber car* you are taking belongs to your driver who is willing to share the ride, as a job, to add more income for his living. He or she also has to cover all costs of expenses such as gas, oil change, AC or brake replacement, winter tires, and all other maintenance and hidden costs. This is why Uber only takes 10% to 30% commission from gross fares that their drivers make. This is why Uber sometimes has to pay out to cover working hours lost under incentives form or downtime. And this is also why the city tries to avoid any more fees and cost applied on drivers (workers) so as to make sure drivers bring home no less than minimum wage.

On some occasions, Uber drivers earn much more than a professional worker or a manager does. A story from the city of Toronto: A few months ago, there was a driver who luckily received an UberBlack call at extremely high surge pricing on a holiday. He earned $860 for less than a one-hour trip from downtown Toronto, up to Brampton. It was not clear if it was because the rider was too intoxicated, or it was a system error. Most engineers find that Uber technology is very advanced and accurate. We rarely see something wrong with the fare auto-calculation via application unless Uber staff tries to adjust or refund the fare to keep their customers happy.

It is also the reason we see no Uber sign on Uber platforms. Uber does hand out Uber stickers, but we rarely see one on an Uber car since many Uber drivers don't want to let people know they are doing Uber. Some Uber entrepreneur drivers also think that they shouldn't have to advertise for free when Uber doesn't pay them to put a sign on.

Overall, Uber is great idea.

If you are looking toward advanced technology such as flying cars or driverless cars, reading the next analysis will be really interesting.

2.3 Driverless cars to replace Uber drivers?

Some media outlets have reported Uber companies claimed to buy at least 500 000 Google or Tesla self-driving and electric cars if they are out to the market in the next few years. In August of 2016, it was in the news again: "Uber to start testing self-driving car in Pittsburgh." Most of us fail to believe that this is possible! Why do people positively think Uber will be able to do that? Well, they look at technology innovation, and Uber's fast growth in the first five years, with more than $60 billion valuation by 2016. However, let's take a look back the ride-sharing company foundation. Uber is a technology company with lead engineers designing and developing the rideshare app. When Uber first started, they refused to be defined as a private transportation company but just an app runner. They were carefully thinking of taking the brutal responsibility of insuring all parties on the road. In fact, they owned NO vehicles. Drivers have to pay for accumulated maintenance and hidden costs over the years. That's easy to understand. Uber was looking for a sufficient amount of funding. Say that Uber is buying 500,000 driverless cars to replace 500,000 driver partners. That means they will take 100% commission instead of 25% from 500,000 drivers. Their revenue is boosted a lot more. However, can this investment's ROI be enough to cover their total costs? Let see what the new investments and monthly costs are when added up:

Assume: Uber pays for 500,000 driverless vehicles. An average Uber vehicle price is at $100,000 (UberX or UberPool may be lower; UberBlack may be more expensive. All fees and tax included). This price is estimated on the next ten years when Tesla or Google engineers have 100% understanding and safe process of the vehicle self-operation (auto turn by turn and all human safety functions are perfectly measured):

Car purchase: $100,000 x 500,000 cars = $50,000,000,000 (50 billion dollars), plus:

Costs:
1. Insurance: 500,000 x $500 = $50,000,000 (= $600,000,000 per year)
2. *Gas: 168 x 5 x 500,000= $420,000,000 (= $ 20,160,000,000 per year)
3. *Car wash: $10 x 500,000 x 365 = $1,825,000,000 per year)
4. *Oil change: $100 x 500,000 x 12 = $ 600,00, 000 per year)
5. Vandalism cost
6. Salaries and compensations for engineers, staff, technicians, and management teams also cost billions of dollars.
7. All other hidden fees, costs, and taxes tend to be extremely high.

*(Gas: assume that all cars are running continuously for 168 hours a week; average five litres for one hour or 50kms; 1 litre for $1)
*(Car Wash: once a day, $10 per car)
*(Oil change: approximately, with max engines 24/7 operation, each

car is supposed to have the oil changed every month, with synthetic oil required)

Now, we don't need to solve the mathematic problem accurately, but we just need to imagine. We can see that when the numbers are added up, there are trillions of trillions of dollars.

There are other realistic factors that make the idea of Uber replacing current Uber drivers with self-driving cars in the next 10 years, impossible: unrecognizable localized routes from riders, vandalism or terrorism, accurate accident reports, unexpected software glitches, safety prompt reaction;, riders' command limitation, etc.

For sure, the head of Uber finance, and investors, have to take all these numbers into account. As I predict, if Uber goes ahead with this new business model, they will go bankrupt right after the first month of operations, even when they go public. The Uber founders and executive management team are adored by this smart business idea (owning no vehicle). It may change and carry out new business models with new management or a new business mindset. The current Uber business has been growing fast in the past few years. There is no reason they would want to risk the investment.

However, there is still concrete hope in our technology and the rideshare service sector. Self-driving vehicles on streets within the next decade is definitely possible technology. Tesla and Google, indeed, have successfully tried it out on highways. Uber is investing millions of dollars at a selected university in doing research for this future innovation and invention. If people think deeply, they would see Uber's strategy in operation and implementation of self-driving cars is essentially feasible! However, there is a catch. Of course, the private multi-billion valued Uber business is unlikely to cover monthly *super-costs* (various, fixed, and hidden) for all their vehicles. But, they can rely on their driver partners and technology. They can apply the same business model to the new era of technology. Time goes by, into the future. People will follow the latest advanced technology. They will start purchasing and replacing their older car models with these newer innovative Tesla, self-driving cars, electrics cars, or natural fuel (solar sun) cars. Uber drivers are among these pioneers to experience this first. With more attractive compensation, benefits and cooperation, they are willing to invest in higher-end vehicles. Again, Uber shall decentralize the ownership to their *independent contractors* as traditional partnership to take over their costs. In return, Uber still stays as a technology incorporation that focuses on investing, designing and developing the rideshare self-driving cars in labs and road testing. There is one more solution for this feasible experiment: leasing. Uber has noticed that leasing is not the best idea for full-time drivers. That could be an alternative choice. Consequently, Uber still owns no car, and we are still likely to experience the new self-driving cars from Uber's driver partners.

2.4 Tipping:

Through our industrial revolution, kicked off in Great Britain in the 1760s, our lives have been improved, and moved from farming to industry. We are now moving to a newer and higher-class stage called the service industry, which includes such things as tourism, music, Hollywood movies, robotics, electronics, sporting events, and entertainment. Tipping is popular and considered as a courtesy in modern western countries such as the USA, Canada, and other countries in the G8. We tip when we pay at a restaurant or a pub. We tip for a taxi driver. We tip for a hairdresser. We tip for a nail technician. Uber drivers are among those who work in the service industry. However, there was tricky language composed by Uber, "No need to tip." Most people, including the most professional and well-educated people, have been lured and misled in the first five years since the Uber launch. Some pioneer Uber drivers had tried to hang a tipping sign in their cars to remind riders that tipping is not included in the fare. However, Uber did not recommend this action. The driver will be reminded and may be deactivated if they repeat this. Riders, who don't support tipping or can't afford it, find it offensive and may rate the driver low. The other reason why most of us hop out of an Uber vehicle without tipping is that the service is automatically done through the app. The moment is too quick to think how much change we have in our wallet so that we can tip. We used to pay taxi drivers in cash and were willing to tip with change or whatever money we had in our pocket. Tipping an Uber driver is so rare that whenever any driver is lucky enough to get tipped, she or he goes to social media forums and tells fellow drivers about their fortune of the working day. The odd, weird thing is that female drivers get tipped more often than male drivers, no matter how the passengers understand the Uber service descriptions!

If you have tipped your drivers well, you may find a story about you here: fb.com/groups/UberToronto

So, why doesn't Uber want their customers to tip drivers? The CEO of Uber, Travis Kalanick, has a mission to make Uber cheaper than a taxi. That's the core value of Uber in order to attract the customers. In many of the United States, Uber has lowered fares to compete with other ridesharing businesses, especially Lyft. After years of business development, his team goes even farther and thinks to take over public transportation. He wants people to feel that taking Uber is as cheap as taking public transit. Therefore, he was worried that tipping would make the fares higher and harder to afford to take one. He wants everybody to be able to afford to take Uber.

Who to tip? A driver on social media shared a story that makes us think deeply about tipping. One day, he came to pick up four secondary school students. When he dropped them off, he was surprised that the boys tipped him. The tip he got for this trip included a few quarters and a loonie. It wasn't a large amount, but the value and meaning was tremendous, and something that he hadn't received for a long time, even when he picked up professional adults such as a VP of a big company, party-goers, or businessmen. The world would be a better place if all adults had honest and purely humane minds, like those of children.

Read story here: www.fb.com/groups/UberToronto

How much, and when should you tip? For those who take Uber every morning to commute to work, and for those who are defined as low-income families, it is not expected that they tip. It is absolutely optional. However, those who go to parties where they spend hundreds of dollars on food and drinks are the ones who are defined as high-income families. Those who are on the way to an airport to take a paid vacation or a covered business trip, and those, generally speaking, who are happy and can afford to tip, should go ahead and tip for your service. Even when you are sad, it may help. There is another story: a woman had a bad day at work, she paid orders for all people in line behind her to make her day better. (The original story here: www.LysonMedia.com). We already appreciate when our driver takes us home, or to work, safely and pleasantly. If you have a bad day, you can share your story to your driver. It may help you feel better at the end of the day. Sometimes, just buying your driver a coffee would mean a lot, and it doesn't feel as though it added to the expense of your trip.

2.5 How does Uber attract more and more drivers?

As we know, surge pricing is playing a very important role in attracting professionals to join Uber platforms. Not all drivers earn the same amount of cash. Some Uber drivers start to learn quickly how to make the most out of the Uber business. They can maximize their average earnings up to $60 an hour, or even more. However, a number of new Uber drivers join but quit fairly soon because they can't make more than minimum wage overall. A few drivers run around for fun, talking and meeting new people. That's why the turnover of partners is significant to Uber. In order to have enough drivers around the town at all times, Uber has been applying for referral campaigns with promotion codes for a long time now. In a typical advertisement, Uber persuades people that driving for Uber will turn their cars into a moneymaking machine. Something like: "Sign up and drive this weekend to bring home hundreds of dollars" (sometimes they even give a specific catchy number). They succeed in getting people who believe that driving for Uber, as a part time job, will make them a good amount of cash. The turnover starts from here. After drivers sign up, they find it is not easy to make that money. Some recognize that they don't have as many benefits as they did in an office job. Moreover, Uber applied algorithm and restrictions that these drivers feel are unfavorable. For example: ten to thirty minute auto-logoff after two missed or cancelled trips. The worst is deactivation of partnership. The other concern is that every year Uber seems to lower fares. Of course, raising or lowering the fare depends on the economy. With the downfall of oil pricing, there is no reason to make it more expensive to ride an Uber. For those who don't drive for Uber, there are some smart tricks that make top drivers earn much more than others, or new driver partners. The reason why Uber put these sanctions on these tricky drivers is because they cause frustration for riders. Some riders find it unreliable. Although Uber is promoting that earning from driving for Uber is a huge source of income on the side, they want people to sign up for a decent-paying job rather than wanting to be on platforms to make a *super-profit* from their business and abuse the system. However, after getting used to the system, some top partners find that what Uber is trying to do is actually helpful and respectful, if she or he knows how to take advantage of it.

2.6 Do longer trips make more money?

Uber drivers get paid in net fare based on distance plus time (The net fare is equal to the gross fare that the passenger pays, minus the Uber commission of 10%-30%, minus the rider fee or booking fee). The economists look at all Uber platforms price catering to appraise the municipal or provincial economy, particularly UberX. By September 2016, the Toronto UberX rate was 0.81cents per kilometer and 0.18cents per minute. A base fare is $2.50. Overall, people think that the longer the trip is, the more money the driver makes. When all the facts are brought in, the answer is: It depends on when and where a partner drives. In Toronto (GTA, Canada), the best time to drive in downtown is during the morning rush hours (5:00 AM till 10:00 AM, the top earning drivers never pick up nonsurge rides at this time), on weekdays, or on holidays and weekend mornings and late evenings.

In the afternoon and evening, Uber drivers are believed to face more condensed traffic. Even when surge pricing is applied, being stuck in rush hour traffic makes drivers spend a lot more time with the same fare. There are more driver partners in the evening than in the morning because they have daytime jobs. Therefore, surge pricing is not as high as during the morning commute.

With high surge pricing, Uber drivers love long trips. One single long trip, for example, from downtown Toronto to Toronto Pearson International Airport, is equal to an Uber driver's earnings from pickups during the entire morning hours. Without surge pricing, around 7AM, accepting a long ride is a disaster to an Uber driver. The partner will be brought away from good surge hours and has to face traffic jams here and there on the Gardener Express or highway 401. It totally ruins his morning! That means short rides are better than long, non-surged rides at this time.

On high-speed limit, suburb, or highway routes, with clear traffic, long rides are much better than short rides because the waiting and pickup time are eliminated. With current earnings being by the minute, Uber drivers prefer taking highways instead of an alley way or streets packed with streetcars, bikes, cars, and pedestrians.

With an interruption of the rating system, Uber riders are given the chance to choose a route that makes them happy. However, for drivers, sometimes a few bucks difference is huge value. The $10 fare that the driver earns in ten minutes is much worthier than the $10 fare that he/she earns in sixty minutes. There should be an understanding of this so that there can be mutual benefit and satisfaction for both riders and drivers.

2.7 Your own boss?

In terms of timing and schedule, it is absolutely flexible and under driver partner control. Uber drivers can pick any time to work in a twenty-four hour day, and any day of the week, month or year. They can choose to work continuously, day and night, without sleeping (in some cities, drivers are strictly advised not to drive more than the specific length of time specified by the city's transportation ministry); or, they can choose to work only a couple of hours per week on their free time.

On the other hand, with the clear mission of Uber's CEO and co-founder Travis Kalanick, the Uber app is occasionally technically updated in favor of riders (Uber's customers). His team is trying to build and maintain a reliable and affordable business model. If they let drivers take full control, and earn too much, the Uber fares would probably be higher than taxi fares. That would be wrong. That goes against Uber's confident slogan, "Uber – Cheaper than a taxi." Uber applies some restrictions and rules on their partners to make sure they follow the company's vision and purpose. This also helps to eliminate some bad partners who frustrate Uber users by not offering five star services.

Recently, UberBlack and UberXL drivers complained that they started receiving UberX requests. That means that they would earn less with their expensive vehicles. Uber explained that this update was done in order to create more trips for these high-end vehicle owners, since the UberX demand is dramatically increasing.

Being your own boss is not possible by working for someone else, or partnering with other businesses. The only way to be your own boss is to start up your own business and have 100% control.

2.8 Driver refuses low-rated pickups:

As we know, the Uber experience is different in every country, culture and economy. We all know that American people are extremely ambitious and competitive. Unlike Americans, Canadians are a little more laid back, and treat each other much nicer. If you have tried Uber both in the USA and in Canada, you may understand that. In the USA, a number of Uber drivers pack their cars with extraordinary service extras such as candy, water, snack, gums, chargers, etc., to maintain high ratings and secure jobs. American Uber driver partners are also picky on who they are picking up. If your rating is somehow too low, for example below three stars, chances are that these drivers will skip you. They think you are a bad passenger who may give them bad rating or a hassle. They doubt your behavior. In fact, they believe that your rating is telling them everything about your personality. You may be seen as a drug dealer, a racist, a high-tempered individual, a disrespectful professional, or a mean rider who doesn't tip. In contrast, Canadian drivers seem to love everyone that gives them a beep (The Uber driver partner's app will be beeping if they receive a call for a ride). Most drivers don't even bother looking at how many stars you have. Some other factors are more important for them than your rating, such as the distance and time from your pickup point, or surge pricing. It doesn't make sense to a driver, twenty minutes away, to go to a pickup point and find out that the passenger just needs a ride for 200 meters. With these short trips, they basically lose money since they don't get paid for the time it takes to pickup point. With high surge pricing, they may not mind taking these short trips, especially in downtown where the city traffic is a headache. At high surge pricing time, like morning rush hour, or on weekends and holidays, UberPools or non-surge UberXs are ignored, or are not a priority. You may be smart and lucky enough to get one, but the excitement of the driver's rate is not as much as that of the surge pricing.

2.9 Why drivers keep driving happily

As we know, Uber's revenue is based on the commission from the fare that drivers get. Driver partners, who signed up to drive before August 2015, get 80% of the gross fare. Those who started after this day, earn 75% of the fare. Uber gets average 20% commission. Say in one hour, an Uber driver has one pickup (one fare). The gross fare is $12.5. Uber gets $2.5 (Rider/booking fee) + $2 (20% from $10 net fare)= $4.5. In this one hour the driver gets paid $8/hour wage. How much does Uber really get from this $4.5? If there is one million Uber vehicles being on route around the world during that hour. In an hour, Uber earns at least $4.5 x 1000 000 = $4.5 million dollars!

The newer drivers also face a lot of fare cuts like we mentioned above. Uber keeps the promotion going, however, and a lot of new people are still registering into the transport system.

They are driving happily, without comparing how much they actually earn to how much the former partners earned. They may be just experiencing the initial excitement.

Lack of education makes the job applications competitive. Uber is entering the industry, and cutting unemployment dramatically. Those who don't have high education or qualifications find it harder to get a good job. While they are waiting for an offer of a dream job, they drive for Uber, part time. It becomes their major income since the waiting time for a dream job is long. The fare, and Uber's cut, is really shocking to them, but they have no choice.

Some drivers joined the company for enjoyment and meeting new people. For them, driving around and seeing the city, during the day and night, is amusing and fun. These partners fall into two categories: freelancers and lovers of travel. They like to be free and flexible. Uber, for them, is the perfect lifestyle.

Some entrepreneurs take advantage of Uber to do business. A realtor, who signed up to drive for Uber, has built up an extensive list of new clients, which he obtained from Uber customers. He said that the earnings from Uber were not necessarily a primary source of income, but what he got from it was huge. Steven Lyson, from Toronto, works for a real estate agency. A couple of years ago, when he learned that Uber had launched in Toronto, and found that Uber would be a potential business gig, he registered to drive, part time. Every week, he meets and introduces his business to hundreds of new people. Thanks to Uber, he has earned $75,000 extra, on top of his annual income, by referring Uber riders to his properties list. The other businessmen are doing the same thing. They have a lot of chances to advertise and sell their products by driving for Uber during their free time.

Read more stories on: fb.com/groups/UberToronto

2.10 Are top Uber partners top earning drivers?

A *top* partner is sometimes misunderstood as being a top-earning partner, but this isn't really true. With Uber, the top partners are those who have the best attitudes and the highest ratings, and the cleanest vehicles. They make an effort to offer a five star service to the city. They are open-minded and are friendly to talk to when you step in their car, and they dress professionally. Some may even offer a snack or water on route. They are also more polite.

Top earning partners are those who are very active on social media forums, which help them to learn all the tricks. They master the Uber system and take advantage of their understanding of how the technology works best for them. Their earnings are unbelievably high. You may be, occasionally, lucky enough to catch these dudes. They are the ones who randomly pop up on the app. You may find them on holidays or during extreme weather alerts. They may be found at night on the weekend. They are just like those rare Pokemons. (*Pokemon Go is the hottest smartphone game, launched in early July 2016. Game players go out in real life, on streets or in public locations, to catch Pokemons, which are animated creatures. The rare Pokemons are hardly ever seen, but, when you do catch them, you are advanced to another level.) Some people appreciate their sudden service. Some hate them since it's a very expensive trip. They really challenge Uber technology to add a stricter update, though they are a factor that periodically boosts Uber revenue.

2.11 Is it safe to take Uber?

Firstly, Uber confidently tells people that they have five million dollars worth of insurance to cover their passenger in case they were to get in a severe accident. Secondly, Uber is a technology; they built a super smart app with enough information to track down anything in the system. In the app, each driver has a clear portrait photo of their face, with address, phone number and credit card information. (Sometimes a credit card is used as an ID to track down personal details of a person.) Uber ratings and reports are strict, and work very well in helping to manage driver and rider behavior and interaction. One may be deactivated under investigation, if breaching any Uber platform policy.

Some people are constantly asking why they should take an Uber when they don't know anything about the driver. Well, this has been answered through chapters in this book. Those people who ask these types of questions are: those who work for a taxi company; those who are taxi drivers' relatives or supporters; those who are resistant to technology and change; those who rarely need a transport service; those who are Uber or rideshare haters.

The difference that they see between a cab and an Uber is that a cab will be of a certain color, and have a sign on the top of it, while an Uber vehicle will be unrecognizable and is operated by an "unknown" driver.

If only they would try taking an Uber, and talking to the driver, they would be convinced that Uber drivers are registered and qualified drivers. (Check out the chart on www.fb.com/UberBook.KevinLy.) They may be a retired grandparent, a college student (must be 21 years of age or older), an entrepreneur, an author, a sister, a brother, a professional, a photographer, a freelancer, a mom...and the list goes on.

An interesting fact: Some former taxi drivers failed to go through an Uber background check when they registered to drive for Uber. If you have a chance to stop by an Uber office, you will see that a lot of taxi drivers are trying to join Uber platforms; especially after new city regulations were applied.

How safe is taking an Uber? Every Uber driver has to pass the currently strict background check. They must have a clear photograph of their face available, in the app, to show riders whenever they order a ride. (Uber is checking occasionally, through the app.) Sometimes, the portraits affect drivers' ratings because the way that they look matters to customers – a friendly smile or a serious face, like a criminal's. Some people do judge the book by the cover! Every Uber driver must have a unique, valid number to contact them with, and it is a significant source of personal data in Canada, the USA, and other countries. Besides that, Uber drivers register with basic necessary information such as a home address, phone number, email, plate number, vehicle make and model, and personal insurance. When a severe incident occurs, information is much more accessible in order to track down an Uber driver than it is for a taxi driver.

So, is it completely 100% safe to take an Uber? It is the same question you would ask regarding any other means of transportation, such as an airplane, a train, a car, a bus, or a subway. Is it 100% safe to go through a green light? (Going through a green light, when someone else goes through the red light in the other direction, is how T-bone accidents happen.) The answer is: Nothing is perfect. Everything is based on trust. Similarly, even if only good individuals owned guns, this would still not ensure us that we would have a completely safe community or society. Every human being has two opposite faces – kindness and anger, happiness and sadness. Imagine when a good and well-educated member of your family, who owns a gun, suddenly becomes stressed out. What would happen when a gun is in the right hands but at the wrong time? An accident may happen anywhere, at any time.

Chances are that you have heard of a few incidents, here and there, involving Uber drivers. Why are they such hot topics? *Uber* and *Donald Trump* are the best examples of the most searched phenomenal words on Google in 2015 and 2016; they are well branded and well known. The media and news sources love talking about Uber or Donald Trump. That way they can attract a huge number of viewers (traffic) to their sites. So, they take every single chance.

Nobody is above the law. The city has no tolerance for any kind of crimes.

Your belief is more important. Why do you have to be so hesitant and resistant, while, across the country, millions of Uber trips have been taken? According to Uber Canada, in a Facebook Post, on June 18, 2016, "147 Uber rides started around the world – tying for our two billionth trip" (Uber Toronto - Canada: fb.com/UberToronto). I hope that this book will exclusively help you to feel better and safer, and to accept and enjoy affordable Uber rides around the town, as well as helping you to follow up and enjoy the convenience of upcoming technology.

Chapter 3: UBER & ITS REFLECTION ON THE ECONOMY

3.1 Do Uber rates drop every spring?

In the past five years, Uber has faced a slowdown every January, just like a retail store does. Riders have spent their money during the statutory holidays. The social events of the season are over, and it is the coldest season in the country, so the riders are likely to stay inside more. With the oil sector and economy interruption, especially the economic recession in 2015 (Chinese stock crash crisis), Uber decided to lower fares in more than 100 cities in the USA and Canada. Overall, the Uber market in Canada is more stable than in the United States of America. In the United States of America, most of the markets no longer have a cancellation fee. (A cancellation fee is a $5.00 penalty to be charged to each rider who does not show up after a driver has been waiting for more than five minutes.)

The Rideshare Dashboard had some data for UberX by January 23, 2015:

There is no longer base fare for the cities: Los Angeles, Dallas, Lincoln, Memphis, Orange County, St. Louise.

Paid time per minute is really low (0.17 cents per minute and under) in the following cities: Albuquerque, Atlanta, Baltimore, Charlotte, Cleveland, Corpus Christi, Dallas, Denver, Detroit, Fresno, Jacksonville, Lexington, Lincoln, Louisville, Memphis, Miami, Modesto, Nashville, Oklahoma City, Orlando, Providence, Raleigh-Durham, Sacramento, Salt Lake City, Spokane, Tampa Bay, Toledo, Tucson, Tulsa, and Virginia-Beach-Han.

Paid per mile is lower (lower than 0.75 cents per mile) in the following cities: Charlotte, Corpus Christi, Detroit, Jacksonville, Lexington, Louisville, Memphis, Nashville, Orlando, Providence, Raleigh-Durham, Spokane, and Toledo."

Why do drivers complain but keep driving?

This data proved that the economy in these regions might not be as strong as others. Or, the unemployment rate is higher than others. (Drivers hardly ever find a better job, so they have to accept a lower paying, part time job for living.) A number of Uber partners are driving while waiting for a new job offer. They feel that earning a few bucks is better than being jobless. Uber may cater the price per mile base on how smooth the traffic is in the city. The infrastructure, and the volume of the highways, in a city also matter in determining the distance charge.

Early in 2016, UberPool was successfully rolled out as an alternative way to lower expenses for the ridesharing users. By taking UberPool, riders save up to 40% when compared to other Uber platforms. However, riders need to be careful about the right place and time to take an UberPool, since its routes are altered and longer by sharing with Poolmates pickups. UberPool is one of the smartest ideas from Uber. It is good for the government and the environment. But, for drivers, UberPool is an unpleasant interruption of their usual great earnings. Even though Uber has some strict *punishments* for Uber drivers who try not to accept UberPool trips, many of their partners are skipping UberPool requests. That's the reason why it takes a lot more time for an UberPool driver to come to pick you up. When a rider orders an Uber, the request goes to the nearest driver in their area. If the request is missed or ignored, it will be passed to the next driver, and then to the next driver, and so on. The one who picks you up is an UberPool friendly driver. It could be one of the *top partners* who tries to keep his record clean with a high rating. Or, basically, it is a fairly new driver who just joined.

It is such a pain and a regret for driver partners in these cities. They drive the same distance but spend a lot more low-paid time. It makes the earning lower in wage per hour. They used to make a lot more with Uber. The social media forums were flooded with complaints and threats to quit from diver members. Some claim they pay to drive for Uber. They start looking for something else that they believe will be a higher paying job – maybe by going back to a 9 to 5 career.

Uber claimed that they cut the fares and rolled out UberPool to encourage people to use the service during an economic downturn or a financial crisis. That would increase the trips and get the surge back to a normal frequency. There is an important fact that once the fare is cut, it is not easy to get it back to the previous rate. Uber has created the fare estimation habit that Uber riders use on a daily basis. So, chances are, that once Uber lowers the rate, they are not going to put the price back up, even though they have convinced their driver partners of this. Uber actually realized the cut would hurt their partners, so they brought in guaranteed earnings in gross fares with acceptance conditions. That means Uber drivers have the difficult option to not drive at all, or drive at a guaranteed rate. (The net earning is usually calculated to be no more than $20.00 per hour, before expenses. *Net fare is the amount that Uber drivers earn after the deduction of the Uber fee and commission.) In an incentive promotion for drivers, Uber uses the term "gross fare" so that Uber drivers feel that their earnings are a high number.

3.2 Uber is great, but why does the taxi still exist?

The taxi service has been severely interrupted since the Uber launch in 2008. With the ridesharing service having better affordability, reliability, and convenience, it has turned out to be more competitive for the traditional taxi monopoly. Several taxi companies, so far, have filed for bankruptcy and closed down. It is a touching moment when we see a cab driver begging to pick someone up in front of Walmart.

People are wondering why there are still some taxi companies operating in their cities. In Toronto, Becks and other taxi companies are still running around the city, along with Uber.

Firstly, as we all know, Uber has surge pricing at peak times. When the price is raised by two times, or higher, 99% of riders can't afford to ride in the available Uber cars that are left at that moment. These Uber vehicles, when in high demand, are saved for whoever understands the value of a rideshare service with private drivers, as it tends to be scarce. In difficult times, the 99% have to take public transit or taxis instead. Furthermore, in order to compete with rideshare pricing, taxi companies have accordingly lowered their fares as well. In chapter 8 (8-2.5), we will discuss more about the rate that applies to Uber riders: 99% are the poor, and 1% are the rich.

The second reason: A taxi randomly and visibly appears right in front of where you are. We all know it just takes a few minutes to request and wait for an Uber, and it's convenient, while it takes 10 to 20 minutes to call a dispatcher and wait for a cab. However, as its service tradition, the taxi drivers keep running and idling around the city to catch passengers on the streets. There are times when some impatient riders just hop in the cab without waiting.

Thirdly, we have to accept that there are a certain number of taxi supporters. Some people are resistant to the change and technology because of their age or personality. The conservative people, who respect their privacy, completely try to avoid opening any social media account. Chances are that these people haven't caught up with how far we are going into the future of technology and innovation. Some of these people haven't heard about Uber or any other rideshare enterprises coming to their town. They don't use private transportation service often, but when they do, they only know to take a cab.

Lastly, which should not be a reason, but there are a few people who never use a credit card or a smartphone for financial security or as a personal privacy. So, they have no way to log on to Uber platforms. Some of them use their family's or friend's Uber accounts instead, although they mostly take a cab.

3.3 Uber has its reflection on the city's technology and economy:

As of August 2016, the service is available in over 66 countries and 507 cities worldwide. However, the Uber story didn't start that easy. Uber launched their first service, called *UberCab*, in San Francisco in 2009. Their service was initially experienced in the strongest and healthiest economic cities. Then, in 2012, they expanded internationally. How soon Uber came to your city could tell how strong your economy was at the moment. It also tells how friendly and open-minded your government is toward the regulations for new rideshare platforms such as Uber or Lyft, or accommodation services such as

Airbnb. Canada has one of the healthiest economies in the world. Canadian banking and healthcare systems worked tightly together to maintain sufficient coverage for businesses and people through both the 2008 and 2015 economic recessions. Toronto was actually voted as one of the best cities to live, work and study in during that time. That's why Toronto was one of the first global economic targets when Uber expanded internationally.

3.4 Uber's surge pricing algorithm and your city:

The frequency of surge pricing could tell you something about where you live. It is literally telling you which part of your city has the richest people living and working there. Indeed, Uber has done the market research and understands all your neighbors in the city.

Of course, the most regular surged area in every city is downtown, but not every corner of downtown is highly surge priced. There are some specific parts of the city that have more surge zones than others. For example, in Toronto, the most surged zones are: Liberty Village in King West Village (located between the Gardener Express and King street West, from Dufferin to Bathurst, with most of the commuting professionals and entrepreneurs, who work in downtown Toronto, residing here), Roncesvalles Village (the square surrounded by Roncesvalles, Dundas, Lansdowne, and The Queensway), Bloordale Village, Little Portugal, Dufferin Grove, Parmerson – Little Italy, Trinity Bellwoods, Entertainment District, The Junction, Yorkville, Leslieville

(Woodbine Beach), The Annex, Corso Italia (St.Clair and Dufferin), Stockyard District (St. Clair-Weston-Keele), and Willowdale (Yonge and Finch). In The United States of America, there are some states and cities that have crazy surges (up to 8.9x). Oklahoma and Las Vegas are among of them. Oklahoma, a midwestern U.S. state, is home to the National Cowboy & Western Heritage Museum. Oklahoma has the Bricktown Entertainment district, which is known for its dining and nightlife. Las Vegas is one of the most famous destinations for tourists. Las Vegas is famous for its 24-hour casinos and most vibrating entertainment spots. Collecting the high surged fares is much easier in these cities than in others where the economy and leisure are not their strengths.

3.5 Uber platforms has reflection on a city's economy:

Unlike American or European developed countries, South East Asian countries, like Vietnam, Thailand, and the Philippines, are developing economies. They have more motorbikes and bicycles than automobiles. The gap between the rich and the poor is huge. It may take decades more for these rural people to experience an UberX in their land. In Ho Chi Minh City, neither Uber nor their drivers own the service vehicles. There is a logistics and transportation company who made a deal in business licensing with Uber to operate the service on behalf of Uber and share the profits in percentage; the drivers are hired. Uber also launched UberMOTO (motorbikes) in these cities to meet with their economic demand and landscape.

In the biggest cities of developed countries such as Toronto, New York, San Francisco, etc., the municipal citizens experience all platforms of Uber service: UberX, UberSUV, UberBlack, UberSelect, UberAccess, and UberEats (UberBike, delivery).

In the cities of developing countries, Uber service is limited and to be expanded based on the progress of their economic growth.

3.6 What Uber services do the cities around the world have?

As of August 24, 2016:

In Toronto (Canada): UberX, UberSelect, UberBlack, UberTaxi, UberAccess (X or XL).

In Hanoi and Ho Chi Minh City (Vietnam): UberMOTO, UberX and UberBlack.

In Tokyo (Japan): Black Car, Black Van, Taxi Lux, Taxi.

In Bangkok (Thailand): UberX and UberBlack.

In Bejin (China): People's Uber +, UberX, UberBlack.

In Rome (Italy): UberLUX, UberBlack, UberVan, UberTour.

In New York (U.S.): UberT, UberPool, UberX, UberBlack, UberRush.

In Rio De Janeiro (Brazil): UberX, UberBlack, UberEnglish.

In Singapore (Singapore): UberX, UberXL, UberExec, ExecLarge and UberTaxi.

In Moscow (Russia): UberX, UberSELECT, UberBlack.

In Mexico City (Mexico): UberX and UberBlack (X or XL sizes).

In Paris (France): UberX, UberGreen, UberBlack, UberVan.

In New Delhi (India): UberGo, UberX.

(For the other cities, please go to facebook.com/UberBook.KevinLy.)

Chapter 4: UBER & ITS VALUE IN THE ECONOMY

4.1 For driver partners:

4.1.a Uber creates jobs:

Even though a number of Uber driver partners are complaining about ongoing fare cuts, strict rules, and policies, most of them have appreciated the opportunity for an easy way to make money during the economic downturn. Those who drive for Uber are in need of flexibility due to their lifestyle or business. Some drivers don't need a career. They just need a current job that fits in their daily schedule. They may be starting a small business. Some already have full-time office jobs but need extra income for their family. Some may be working for Uber while looking for a dream job. Driving for Uber is considered to be one of the most flexible jobs. You may choose to work at night or in the daytime. You may choose to workday time or nighttime. You may choose to work one hour a week or 24 hours a day. You are allowed to log into the system whenever you are ready to drive. Driving for Uber is also one of the easiest and quickest jobs that you can apply for, as long as your background is clean. Basically, you just download the app, sign up, and provide some necessary personal information. Then you just have to go to the office and watch the orientation video for about ten to twenty minutes. You are also required to sign a paper at that time and provide photo ID. Then it takes a few days to wait for your background and criminal check. Meanwhile, you are asked to upload your insurance, driver license, safety standard certificate, and your vehicle images. You are good to go online right off the bat if you are activated in the Uber computer system. Everything you do is monitored through the app, such as your behavior, the paid net fare, the fee, etc. In some other busy cities, new drivers are trying to join but have to be put on a waitlist. Locally, Uber is accepting more and more new driver partners, though they have more than enough. The more drivers Uber has in place, the better for Uber because they don't have to worry about the lack of workforce supply during peak times such as holidays or when there is bad weather.

4.1.b Drivers have a lot of chances to pick up girlfriend/boyfriend:

Of course, like other professional workplaces, trying to reach out to customers on Uber platforms for private personal purposes is prohibited and may lead to deactivation. However, under normal circumstances, a good relationship may be formed from good conversation between a driver and a passenger. Being an Uber driver means that you will log in and go online at peak times to have more pickups. Every day, drivers pick up different people. Some people are professionals who commute to work every morning. Some are heading to bars for dinner or drinks. Some are beautiful, single people. Some are artists. Some are strippers. Some are dancers. Some are foreign tourists. Some drivers even share stories that they have met a lot of prostitutes or sex workers. By talking and asking questions about personal, career, and mutual interests, single drivers have a lot of chances to meet their favorite other half.

Read love stories on: fb.com/groups/UberToronto

4.1.c Part time partners increase their leads for other businesses:

As we now know, some Uber drivers are entrepreneurs or owners of small businesses. The reason that they drive for Uber is to introduce their product and company to their new clients (Uber passengers). Uber warns drivers that soliciting or promoting their business on Uber trips may lead to a low rating. But this doesn't stop them from doing it. With clever talk and sales skills, they obviously can handle situations and maintain a good rating. It's their own vehicle, so they have a right to do it. We have heard the story about the realtor who earned thousands of dollars on top of his earnings made by driving for Uber.

Read successful partners' stories on: fb.com/groups/UberToronto

4.2 For riders:

It is no longer the time when we have to sit in a taxi and have our heart beating fast from watching the fare metre moving, especially when it stops at the traffic lights. We felt that it was very expensive every time we took a taxi in those old days. Thanks to Uber, they bring technology to our era. It is a great business idea, providing great savings for customers, and a great income for smart drivers. UberX is much cheaper than a taxi. With UberPool, people feel like they are taking public transit but in a private vehicle. It is has even more value if you compare it to a business man's private driver. You have to pay a salary to a private driver, both for working and nonworking time. But, with Uber, you pay only when you take it, with an absolutely affordable price, and you are trouble free from owning a vehicle.

The groups of consumers that benefit the most from Uber innovation are those who live or commute to downtown for work. They used to have to pay for expensive parking and insurance. (The urban residents are paying higher insurance compared to rural residents.) Now they can pass all the costs to drivers. They no longer have to worry that the parking has expired, or that they will get a ticket.

Uber has successfully brought us the convenience of our technological generation that we deserve to take part in – The pick up times are an average of five minutes; we can track exactly where our driver is by looking at the map; we can text or call our driver; we can see a photograph of our driver; we can estimate how long it will take to get to the destination and how much it will cost. With UberPool trips, we can even pay the exact estimated price ahead of time! In some cities, Uber is applying this upfront fare on UberX as well. So, no matter which route driver takes, we pay exactly at the estimated amount.

Even with surge pricing, people still prefer taking Uber over a taxi because they feel more comfortable somehow, and, somehow, more important. It is easier for them to break the ice because they know that Uber drivers are in the same industries or professions as they are. Other people feel important because some drivers actually drive fairly new cars. You would love the moment that a clean and shiny black car arrives in front of your house to pick you up and take you to an event or a business trip. You sit in the back and cross your legs like a boss.

Uber is a great choice in avoiding drinking and driving. We used to worry where to park our car, or who would bring our car home if we got drunk. We used to have anxiety over getting caught or pulled over, if we decided to drive home after having some drinks. Now, Uber has solved this problem!

4.3 For the city:

4.3.a Uber creates jobs:
By the end of 2015, Uber had added 8,000 jobs for Torontonians. By May of 2016, Uber has claimed to have added 15,000 full time and part time jobs for the people of the city. Uber has helped to reduce the unemployment rate for the economy since they stepped in.

4.3.b Uber has solved parking, and the headache of owning cars
Since the first day in office, Toronto Mayor, John Tory, has made it a priority to keep the traffic moving smoothly. The city has since clamped down on illegally parked vehicles. The commuters, going to work, find it harder to find a place to park their car on Toronto streets,

so they decide to take Uber as an alternative mode of transportation, and leave the problems to the drivers to deal with.

4.3.c Uber is following the city's development plan:

UberPool is an example of understanding how the city takes the problem seriously, especially with public health and safety, and environment protection. In fact, Toronto is one of the largest cities in the world and is leading in going *green* for the environment, and caring so much about climate change. The city regularly reminds the commuters to carpool or take public transit to reduce pollution. The other solution that Uber commits to the city is to have their drivers regularly inspect their vehicles in terms of emissions or safe engine operation.

4.3.d Economy growth and technology up-to-date:

Along with giant corporations, Uber (fast growing startup) plays an important role in improving the city's economy. Having Uber come so soon to Toronto signals that Toronto is one of the healthiest and most developed cities in North America. As a mayor, John Tory set businesses and startups in technology and innovation as the top priority to keep the city up-to-date and powerful. The mayor had tried to find solutions with councilors to keep rideshare available in Toronto so that people have choices and follow the technology speed.

4.3.e DUI/DWI:

Drinking and driving is one of the most serious problems in Ontario. It is also a major problem in other provinces and states. More than 35% of annual crashes involve D.U.I/DWI (Driving Under Influence, or Driving While Intoxicated). Drivers who illegally operate their vehicles after drinking or using drugs kill people. Since Uber came to the city, the number of deaths due to this kind of impaired driving has been dramatically reduced. People find it affordable and safer to take Uber. Uber gives them peace of mind when they leave their vehicle at home. People who take Uber enjoy partying more than people who drive to a party or an event. In fact, they can drink as much as they want without worrying about the percentage of BAC (Blood Alcohol Concentration).

Chapter 5: UBER & ITS EFFECT
(on partners, riders, and the city)

5.1 How driving for Uber affect drivers?

Since Uber came to the city, the unemployment rate has been dramatically reduced. Uber creates seasonal, part time, and full time delivery and driving jobs for thousands of local people, at both the legal working age and that of the retiring generation. However, nothing is perfect. Like other occupations, driving has positive and negative effects on Uber drivers.

5.1.a Driving affects the mental health of drivers:

Not only driving for Uber, but also driving in general (driving for personal purposes, for a taxi company, or for public transit) also affects a driver's health (physical and mental) conditions.

Hitting the road means that we have to take part in a complicated city traffic system, and deal with all types of drivers. Uber drivers not only have to deal with crazy or impatient drivers on busy streets, but also with different behaviors from riders, which could make their driving job a hassle and a headache. Driving downtown, working during busy peak times (rush hours), and chasing high surge pricing are the most challenging things for an Uber driver. Traffic is slower. The city has recently redesigned the streets to get more bike lanes. More and more limitations on left and right-turns during specific times, as well as construction almost everywhere in the city, make the pickups more difficult and frustrating. Nevertheless, Uber formed a strict deactivation policy, and cut the fares in more than 100 cities in past years, which shocked and frustrated their driver partners. In the United States of America, there were several serious incidents, which occurred on Uber trips that had brought attention to millions of people around the world. Here are the two most infamous reports from the media:

1. Global News report: Taco Bell executive, Benjamin Golden, 32, of Newport Beach, was arrested in November and charged with misdemeanor assault and battery for allegedly hitting driver Edward Caban, 23, on October 30th in Costa Mesa, in Orange County. (You can watch the video here: fb.com/LysonMedia)

2. Reuters report: Jason Dalton, 45, is charged with shooting eight people, killing six of them, on February 20th, in between driving customers for the Uber car service in Kalamazoo, Michigan, about 150 miles (240 km) north of Detroit.

(You can watch the video here: fb.com/groups/UberToronto)

Therefore, Uber drivers need to work smart to relax, keep their behavior under control, take it easy, and let it go, if possible, to avoid road rage or frustration.

Driving for hours may also affect a driver's physical health. For full-time drivers who work long hours, day and night, recklessly, it may cause muscle pains and stress. Make sure you take enough time to rest and exercise regularly to refresh your biological clock and vision condition. Uber drivers don't need to work out for long hours. About 10 to 30 minutes a day, and regularly, is enough. On sunny days with high UV indexes, you need to put on sunblock cream or cover your skin and protect your eyes from the sunlight. Exposing your skin and eyes to the UV rays may cause severe diseases like skin cancer. In the cold winter, Uber drivers need to prepare to keep their body warm and comfortable at all times. The weather may change suddenly. In Canada, temperatures may drop or go up quickly throughout the day. Most of the time, Uber drivers stay in their vehicle, so taking some breaks, and stepping out for a walk, are very important to intaking enough oxygen. Modifying the AC and ventilation system accordingly in their vehicle is also crucial since the air in the busy downtown, and the air in rural surroundings, is different. The more Carbon Dioxide you inhale from other vehicles, the more harmful to your body and health in the long term.

5.1.b Driving styles show Uber drivers' personalities:

Uber drivers have different educations and backgrounds. Their behaviors and personalities are not the same. The way they think and act toward their customers is also different. The way Uber drivers drive could tell us if they are calm, crazy, or bad drivers. Uber drivers who cut through the lines, pass any vehicle ahead, make a sudden U-turn, move the car out of the parking lot in the middle of moving traffic are *taxi style* drivers. This behavior has resulted from their long time service in their career. Every day they pick up different passengers; mostly riders who live in the downtown where people are impatient and in a hurry. They think these actions would help to please these passengers. Over time, it forms a typical driving behavior of cab drivers. Uber has better and tighter management, with a smarter tech process, so most Uber drivers are able to have a better customer service experience. In fact, your driving style can tell whether you are a patient and calm person, an indecisive person, a successful entrepreneur, or just an aggressive individual. These behaviors could reflect on a driver's rating.

5.1.c Driving affects drivers' behavior:

We have learned that driving types could reveal Uber drivers' personalities. That's subjective cause. When a professional who moves from working in an office to driving around, he or she is somehow affected by the job. These Uber drivers are making a huge change in their career. They are switching from daily base tasking habits to challenging adventures. It doesn't apply to all, but they are moving from a comfort zone to physical and mental risks. Some believe earning from driving for Uber is easy money, and fun. That's true. It is part of the good side of this job description. Every day you go out, get extra cash on top of your income, talk to different people, learn a lot of things, and see the city changing from day to night. On the contrary, the more you hit the road, the more chance you will have unexpected accidents or unpleasant incidents. For some Uber drivers, they just learn things around them and aren't affected due to their natural instinct. They started with basic driving skills at the beginning and then adapted to the sophisticated environment. The surroundings make them happy on good days because the other traffic participants are nice and yield the right of way. They get stressed out and frustrated by the mistakes or crazy unexplainable moves made by other vehicles. Multi-tasking while driving, having ups and downs, and lucky or bad luck days for earning, as well as dealing with unpleasant riders' behaviors are other factors that stress them out. For those top driver partners, the only thing we know about them is that they are working smart and are being picky. However, they are the *victims* who are most affected by the Uber operation. They chase the surge. They spend time figuring out how the application really works in order to get the best out of it. They feel extremely excited and happy when they earn high surged fares. They are totally upset and angry when they spend the whole day or night waiting for something good, but it ends up being so *dead*. The surge, appearing and disappearing, drives them crazy with regret. Sometimes they are proud to tell their family that they drive for Uber and earn as much in a day as other general labor workers earn in a week. On bad days (Uber dead time – not many rides, too many new drivers, no surge at all), they log on in hopes of something good, but only end up bringing home regrets or anger because they could only make one good fare that day. Basically, they call it a negative day in earning. They lose money because that single short fare can't cover the mileage and gas they use to drive to a busy zone (downtown), and on the way home the gas gauge is on empty. They experience the extreme highs and lows of excitement and disappointment. People can't see or hear quiet Uber cars on busy streets, but sometimes they do scream, swear, and yell out inside their moving vehicle. Their mind is temporarily noisy and vibrating. Over time, the unstable moods cause behaviour damage. These Uber drivers need to practice, do enough exercise or meditation, take enough rest, find extra joyful activities or motivation enough for them to rehabilitate from driving. Otherwise, they could take it out on innocent people.

5.1.d Uber has changed a number of their partners' lives:
We have all gone through several economic crises. The economic recession financially affects the people and their countries in both microeconomic and macroeconomic levels at the same time. For the macroeconomic problems, the exports and imports are temporarily interrupted; businesses may face job cuts or layoffs. The negative effect could result in bankruptcies or closures for the enterprises. People lose jobs and have to sell their houses, which could cause family problems such as domestic violence, homicide, or suicide. Uber

first rolled out their service in 2008. During the operation period 2008-2016, Uber, along with the economy, has gone through a few critical financial recessions, especially the most recent ones, which involved the Russian Financial Crisis in 2014, and the Chinese Stock Market Crash in 2015. During the hard times, the rideshare service amazingly maintained a moderate number of casual, part time, and full time driving jobs, available for people who lost their jobs or were temporarily unemployed.

The next part of this chapter will compare the affects that Uber has on drivers and riders.

5.2 How does Uber affect riders?

5.2.a *No tipping* culture

With tricky language usage, and the convenience of the app, Uber has successfully generated a *no tip* culture, even in the largest American cities and states. People understand that the rideshare business is categorized as part of the service sector, but Uber drivers are rarely tipped. Riders experience a cashless service. *Cashless* is also misunderstood as *tipless*! The service may be so convenient that people hop in and hop out in seconds, without taking enough time to check if they have enough money to tip their drivers. Uber succeeded in creating an affordable passenger transportation service for all classes in society with their classified product and service categories. Especially, since UberPool was rolled out, the low-income family is the class that has appreciated the service the most. With a no tip culture, they feel that the service is inexpensive, and use the service more often than before, when a taxi was the only choice for a quick private service.

5.2.b Convenience of new technology:

Uber is one of the most convenient technological services and products that have been brought to people. Through the app, we can do and see anything. We see the face of the person who is going to pick us up. We see the estimation for the cost of the fare and the time. We know approximately how much the trip will cost us. We see the chosen route on the maps. We see where our Uber car is. We can contact our driver by calling or texting. We can rate our drivers and maybe leave a comment about their service. We can have our favorite service options based on our financial budget, capacity, and events. Requesting a rideshare car is just one tab away.

5.2.c Entrepreneurs and celebrities no longer need their own drivers:

Before Uber was *born*, entrepreneurs and celebrities used to spend money on an expensive, fancy vehicle, and hire their own private drivers. The costs are huge. They have to pay for their car's maintenance and all other expenditures. Hiring a private driver costs them at least $50,000 annually. Nowadays, Uber technology and convenience are leveled up to the max. The rideshare service is available anytime, day or night, with sufficient options that suit your needs and budget. Entrepreneurs and celebrities need only to request their most favorite and reliable ride through their Uber app, and pay per ride. Justin Bieber, the Canadian famous singer and superstar, has admitted to using the service. They are totally happy that Uber has helped them remove the hassle of owning an expensive car and a private driver.

5.3 How does Uber affect the city?

One of the actions that Mayor John Tory promised to take in the election, to improve the city of Toronto, was to invest sufficiently in technology and innovation in order to stimulate more and more startups and small businesses. The city's votes to legalize Uber, and welcome other smart computerized applications into the city, proves that the city is well prepared and ready for any technology disruption or challenge. Torontonians want their city to be more attractive to tourists, international students, business investors, and skilled workers.

Chapter 6: UBER & THEIR DRIVERS

6.1 Is UBER one of the BEST 100 EMPLOYERS?

A number of businesses and franchises carry out a lot of practice to achieve the title: "The Best 100 Employers" in the country. With this title, they can attract more talented workers and look positive to their consumers. Uber found that it is difficult to be nominated or be voted as one of "The Best 100 Employers."

The billionaire, Richard Branson, Virgin Mobile's founder, has a clear business philosophy: "Clients do not come first. Employees come first. If you take care of your employees, they will take care of your clients." Unlike the way Branson does things, Uber CEO, Travis Kalanick, is running his business with different ethics. The most significant reason why people take Uber is its pricing competition. Despite the occasional surge pricing, the normal fare rate is unbeatable. Uber has to bring on a technology advantage to implement the transportation affordability and convenience. This causes a lot of restrictions and affects driver partners' earnings markup. Uber is willing to deactivate their partners if they find out that their partners have done something harmful during their customer service experience, with or without investigation or evidence. Uber rarely removes a rider account from the platforms, except for those extremely serious problems. If a rider complains, Uber may review, refund, or adjust the fare without calling or notifying their driver partners for dispute or debate. That is why the Uber app does not show the fare right after the trip is ended. It always says, "The fare is being calculated…" Really? A technology company can't process the fare calculation promptly?! The fact is, Uber drivers have to wait until the riders see the fare to see if there is any dispute regarding it. The fare adjustments are secretly done a few days after the trips, if reported, so Uber drivers are unaware of the process. It could be the Uber driver's fault (i.e. a bad route choice), or it could be just to please an Uber customer, to create good customer service experience. Uber has been taking advantage of this practice to prevent spending on refunding. An Uber product manager is hired to take responsibility for creating and implementing a good rider experience by all means.

In some disappointed Uber drivers' eyes, and according to their beliefs, Uber has to change and make more of an effort to improve on partnerships with drivers in order to work toward their potential award title: "One of The Best 100 Employers." Uber may claim that Uber drivers are just independent contractors (partners). They may be treating their office staff (their "real" employees) better. However, they are the first and direct parties used to employ and recruit their drivers with their own management and employment process.

Not until earlier in 2016, has Uber showed positive progress toward their driver partners by topping up UberX drivers' earnings and subsidizing UberPool. Uber riders (Uber customers or passengers) have been wondering how Uber drivers survive on the cheap fares. This is the answer for them: Though the fares are lowered, Uber driver partners get paid almost the same as usual. Uber secretly covers the loss. As a result, Uber lost 1.27 billion dollars in the first half of 2016. Uber is always working to find the best business practice so that every party, including the business itself, is happy.

6.2 Two co-founders with two different cares and interests:

Uber was co-founded by two businessmen, Travis Kalanick and Garrett Camp. However, they have different ethics in doing business. The CEO has a clear mission to make Uber more and more affordable for everyone to take as an alternative to public transit, while the co-founder has some solid concerns about partnerships and operation teams. They have sometimes asked each other to make sure their individual beliefs and actions are acceptable regarding business concerns. In the first few years of start-up, Uber strongly believed in doing everything they could to stand on the customer's side. They have followed the rule: "The customer is always first." We could see this by their upset driver partners, through social media forums and protests. They have gone through so much criticism from both outsiders and insiders. It wasn't until 2016, that Uber started paying more attention and taking more care toward their *independent contractors* (their driver partners). Probably, the feedback from partners took a lot of time and effort to reach the top executive team, but the attention finally has been brought to the head office. They must change! It's hard to have a perfect business model system, but all parties matter.

6.3 UberPool: A great economic idea?

There are two reasons why Uber rolled out UberPool in early 2016. UberPool is the service that appeals to the city's environment activities, to fight climate change, by reducing pollution and solving the city biggest issue: traffic congestion during rush hours. The other reason is that UberPool implementation is part of a solution to reduce the fare as low as possible. From the beginning, when rolling out UberPool, Uber had a mass promotion for it. It has a code called "UberPool2Win." This code pops up every time riders open the Uber app, to encourage them to use Uber, and save more money. At first, with Uber's fascinating and logical descriptions, Uber drivers had expected that UberPool would be such a great potential source of income with "endless" trips. Even tougher, each rider pays up to 40% less than an UberX; Uber claims that driver partners earn more fares. Uber gets 30% commission from gross fares for UberPool matched trips. If they are not matched trips, Uber only charges a 10% Uber fee from driver partners. UberPool only works the best when trips are completely matched, when all four riders step into the four doors, five-seater car, take the same route (longer route, greater earnings), and get off at exactly the same time. That is perfection and ideology. It is never true in real life. Uber does have a similar platform called *UberHop*, but this service is only available at a certain time (rush hours), at certain pickup points (applied in downtown only). In fact, riders, who don't know each other, take different routes in their specific necessary time frame. Some UberPool trips are too short to match with other riders. Some long UberPool trips have a short matched connection.

In addition, it takes a lot of time for Uber drivers to go and pick up the riders in different directions. We all know Uber drivers get paid a little for their working time; particularly Uber drivers almost aren't paid for timing with UberPool. Recently, Uber applied more and more promotions for UberPool, such as making flat fares for UberPool trips, or a $6.00 flat fare for a downtown commute. That means Uber pre-estimates the fare based on the most standard routes and timing. Uber charges the customers with that basic estimation. Some Uber driver partners doubted that Uber selected the cheapest or shortest routes. When it comes to UberPool, Uber GPS direction is mandatory. There are no other choices like on UberX. Consequently, Uber drivers make less money from UberPool than on UberX, or others. UberPool does interrupt Uber partners' income in a hard way. That's why many Uber drivers skip, ignore, or try to miss the UberPool requests. Some UberX drivers are smartly cheating. They take advantage of 10% commission on UberPool unmatched trips. They only accept UberPool trips in surge pricing, and with just the first rider. After Uber learned about this weird strategy from their partners, they updated the application with "automatically added next Pool requests" enforcement. Once Uber drivers accept an UberPool trip, the next incoming request from the second or third riders, and so on, will be automatically added in the app for the driver to pick up. Uber does have an option attached so that the driver can "stop receiving next requests." But, once accepting the UberPool, chances are that the driver will not be fast enough to go to the option to "stop receiving next requests" right away. This matter is creating hesitation in accepting UberPool trips among these smart drivers. They are worried that the second rider will be quickly added as soon as they accept the first one. A driver shared in the Uber Toronto forum (fb.com/groups/UberToronto) that he recently refused to take an UberPool at 3X surge pricing due to the new "automatically added" policy. It is easy for Uber to reduce or partly cover UberPool fares, but it is absolutely not that easy to find a way to compensate enough for the lost income those Uber drivers are facing.

6.4 Why does Uber have a large employment turnover?

First of all, driving is at a high risk of accidents. People admit driving on the road is very dangerous, especially in bad weather and conditions. According to WHO report, nearly 1.3 million people die in road crashes each year, on average 3,287 deaths a day around the world. In fact, driver partners' families do not support the job completely, even though earning is brutally the main factor for this job submission.

Secondly, driving for Uber is never defined as a career. Uber calls their driver partner's independent contractors. That means drivers have to be responsible for all of their own expenditures. Uber has been creating hundreds of thousands of jobs in our country, but the full-time job rate is very small. With that fact and agreement, Uber drivers can't expect any compensation or benefits for health care, parenting leave, seniority, unionization, vacation, etc. A driver member from an Uber social media forum said he left the job because he couldn't find any coverage for dental care. His wise tooth has been pulled out for years, but he is still struggling to find insurance coverage for it. Working for Uber doesn't offer that. He left the job for that reason.

Thirdly, most driver partners consider driving for Uber as a temporary or part time job. Uber comes to the cities to reduce the unemployment rate dramatically. Even though it is just a temporary solution for the long-term matter, the government praises Uber for playing an important role in its economy. Having awareness of the job conditions, people are afraid to consider Uber as their career. A number of Uber drivers are unemployed individuals looking for professional careers. They are driving Uber to pay bills while searching and waiting for a better job offer. As soon as they get the offer, they may quit driving for Uber or make it as a secondary source of income on their free time. It also depends on the demand of the service in the city at the time. If the demand is still high and Uber still keeps the fare at a moderate rate, chances are that these Uber drivers will have strong loyalty and interest in enjoying the driving job on the side. Similarly, some startup entrepreneurs have to stop driving since they get busier with their growing business. In spite of their down times, internally and externally, while driving for Uber, most Uber drivers are, inside their hearts, appreciating that Uber has helped them overcome financial struggle in the difficult times.

Despite different business ethics, Uber's CEO, Travis Kalanick, and his team, agree with Mr. Branson's business philosophy. Uber driver partners are those who stay on the front line to represent the Uber customer service experience and defend its reputation. Learning from feedback and outcomes will help Uber reform the organization regime in justice and diversity. When being well treated, Uber drivers will take good care of Uber customers (riders/passengers) to keep the city moving safely, day and night.

For other reasons, go to: fb.com/UberBook.KevinLy

6.5 Tipping could help cover Uber drivers' lost earnings:

Since the beginning, Uber has made it clear that its vision is to make Uber more and more affordable for everyone to take. Tipping their drivers would make the fare actually higher which goes against the service they provide. By cleverly using tricky language, Uber has successfully persuaded riders not to tip their drivers: "Everything included," "No need to tip," or "Cashless experience." The riders read the language statement without doing the calculation and think in a completely different way: "Tip is already included in fare!" The drivers have felt that this action is dishonorable and misleading. Over time, this practice becomes misconception, habit, or culture. The riders just take a ride and easily hop out of Uber cars – and just say, "Goodbye." They believe the application has done everything automatically by itself. Tipping could have helped to boost the Uber driver's income. Uber wouldn't have to spend a lot of money on begging new drivers to come on board, day by day. It would be actually one of the most attractive jobs with potentially high pay. If Uber had a different way of thinking, they would have done it easily by building a tipping option in the app. However, it is not an easy mathematical problem for Uber to solve since their active rivals keep being born and are growing competitively, such as Lyft, GrabTaxi, Ola, Academy City, InstaRide, Didi, etc. The strongest strategy for Uber to use to beat these enemies, is pricing. Uber doesn't hesitate in cutting the fare down to the lowest level as possible so that no one can compete. Uber has the ability to do that. They keep spending and attracting more and more drivers. It seems like their recruiting is endless. The more drivers they have, the more limitations they can place on the rivals and their partners (whom they call contractors).

6.6 How much does an Uber driver earn?

The most interesting question that every rider wants to know is: How much does an Uber driver really earn per hour? The answer to the question is that there is NO specific answer to this question. Some riders are curious to know how much an Uber driver earns per hour. They insist on requesting the answer, so probably every Uber driver gives them a different number. Driving for Uber is one of the most flexible and casual jobs in the market. Every Uber driver registers to drive for different reasons and earning levels. The earnings are various, high or low, based on time, intelligence, cleverness, knowledge, purpose, and chosen platforms. They are divided into two categories: *low income* (the newbies and the dummies) and *high income* (the top earning driver partners).

The Newbies and Dummies: "Newbies" are new Uber drivers who have just registered and have been approved to drive for the first time. "Dummies" are drivers with a low IQ. It takes quite a long time for dummies to learn the basic tricks for driving and earning. Both "newbies" and "dummies" have low earnings per hour in comparison with other experienced Uber drivers. A number of "newbies" and "dummies" miscalculate their earnings or have no idea how much they make per hour at all. It takes quite a long time for these low IQ drivers to learn the routes, understand the city, and figure out how to earn as much as the top earning driver partners. They hit the road at a time that the experienced drivers would believe to be a really bad time to drive. Some of these drivers are called *"The Top Uber Partners"* by Uber (A top partner is different from a top earning driver). In fact, the "newbies" and "dummies" accept all trips, whenever they are online, to keep their acceptance rate high and make a good impression on Uber. The "dummies" are either self-satisfied drivers or slow learners, and are also resistant to change. After the new rideshare regulation was applied, more and more former taxi drivers who used to be protesters against Uber came to the Uber office to sign up and drive for Uber! As we know, taxi and Uber are two different business models of passenger transportation. Taxi's fare meter runs at a higher price for time and millage, so whenever they get a call, they appreciate it. Sometimes they have to fight to catch a passenger on the streets. When these cab drivers join Uber platforms, they think Uber is just the same as a taxi. Every single Uber request makes them feel happy. Indeed, they don't miss out on anything. They run their cars constantly, putting wear and tear on them, day and night regardless of traffic jams. Let's do an easy and simple math equation for a fare to see how the "newbies" and "dummies" think:

Assume an UberX driver from this category accepts a trip on a busy city street during rush hour, with slow moving traffic, to drive a passenger from the west end of downtown Toronto to the east end of the city. The rider refused to take the express highway. The gross fare is $20 for 60 minutes. It looks like $20 per hour; sounds good, right? The driver complained about the traffic, but was still happy with the fare. They look at the number and think that they should be happy and appreciate it. They think it is better than nothing, or better than working in a fast food restaurant for minimum wage. Here is the answer that proves how much they really earned from this $20 gross fare:

Uber Driver Net Earning:

Uber fee (Uber commission) = 25% = $5
Rider fee (Booking fee)   = $2.5

Net fare = Gross fare – (Uber fee + rider fee) = $20 – ($5+$2.5) = $12.5 (per hour)

As of the end of 2016, will this Uber driver still earn more than minimum wage?

How much does the Uber driver really earn from this net fare:

Realistic earnings= Net fare –(gas + km + various costs + pickup time)

In this case, we could estimate that gas costs the driver at least $5 more for driving 20 kilometres for 60 minutes. These drivers feel that 20 kilometres is not big deal. However, the fact is: the more mileage they put on a vehicle, the less value the vehicle has. When they sell their car, they sell it for less. Pickup time: Uber drivers spend an average of 15 minutes going to pick up a rider. This means that they don't get paid for those 15 minutes or working time. The pickup time is also quite different in other cities and territories. We literally have analyzed and proved that these "newbies" and "dummies" earn less than a minimum wage, at least in this case.

Sometimes the top earning drivers find that these drivers are annoying because these drivers interrupt their good earning time. On the contrary, Uber and riders really appreciate these drivers. Uber continues to recruit these drivers to keep a certain amount of drivers on the streets to make the service available at all times, and to bring down the surge during the peak time. Riders from low-income families are grateful to these drivers as well. If riders are smart and patient, they can request non-surged trips, at peak times, from these drivers.

The Top Earning Partners: They are those who have a higher IQ. They are really smart. Normally, these drivers are freelancers, entrepreneurs, or start-up founders. They don't need a career. They just need a flexible job to pay off the bills and save enough for their funding, vacation and housing. Their earnings from driving for Uber are pretty good. It is not hard to recognize these smart drivers. They are the drivers who picked you up at 5X the rate on Christmas or New Year Eve. They are the ones who picked you up in the middle of nowhere, during rush hour and peak time. After a while of working for Uber, they occasionally trade their cars in to get a new one. They work smartly and humbly, and then are able to have vacations with family. Some drive UberBlack or other high-end platforms. How can they afford to buy these vehicles? The answer is simple– they are investing. They buy expensive cars, but, in return, they earn much more. They are very active on social media platforms, and listen and learn from pioneers, other drivers and riders. (You can meet and talk to them here: fb.com/groups/UberToronto.) They are aware of everything to do with the rideshare business. They are the ones who do the math (above) before taking the rides. They set out their standard pickups with high fares (Some claim that they earn an average of $60 per hour). By earning high fares, they can save enough for the incurring expenses. They are the ones who go on the facebook groups and show the expensive fares, with less driving time and mileage. The "newbies" and "dummies" find this impossible. For Uber, these drivers are their favorite targets to put more restrictions on, while appreciating their ability to boost Uber's super-profit, periodically throughout holidays and seasons.

6.7 What has Uber done for their driver partners?

Even though it is quite a long way for Uber to resolve all partnership concerns to become one of "The Best 100 Employers", Uber has done numerous good things for their driver partners over the years. Uber's CEO, Travis Kalanick, has admitted that Uber drivers play a very important role in Uber's success. He knows that his superior consumer care is not always perfect, and might be hurting his partners somewhere. To make sure that everything is running fairly well in the service mechanism, Uber has brought excellent operation managers on board, who are hired to listen and take care of driver partners and fleets. The following favors that Uber has successfully attempted have been recognized by their driver partners and media:

6.7.a Guaranteed gross fare:

The guaranteed gross fare is usually applied in the spring when the fares are cut due to slow consumption after the Christmas and New Year holiday season. That is when Uber drivers complain about *dead time* (slow or low demand). Like manufacturing workers facing an annual layoff period, Uber drivers stop, or limit, their driving time to avoid the shortage of coverage for the costs. They may look for a temporary job to make up the difference at this time. To support and encourage their drivers to keep driving, so as to balance the demand-supply for affordable fare pricing, Uber kicks in the guaranteed driving hours package, with some conditions. During this season, if a driver goes online (to drive) from 7am-9am, or 4pm-6pm, accepting all requests, he or she will be qualified for the guaranteed promotion if they make less than the guaranteed rate. For example, the guaranteed rate is $25 per hour. If an Uber driver makes $20 per hour, Uber will keep their promise to top up the driver's earnings to $25 per hour. There is a catch, however. It is the gross fare. If the driver needs to know how much they really earn, they need to scroll up and do the math (Uber Driver Net Earning, Chapter 6 part 6 "How much does an Uber driver earn?"). Overall, this guarantee is somehow good for a number of partners who keep driving during this difficult time. It is safe to opt in to avoid earning far less than a minimum wage paying job.

6.7.b UberPool savings:

More and more riders start taking UberPool trips nowadays. Uber knows that they have successfully encouraged a lot of people to take UberPool. Uber claims that it is part of making the service more affordable and boosting demand.

In downtown Toronto, Uber has set a flat $6 fare for any UberPool trip taken within a designated city area. That means your short UberPool trip is as cheap as a TTC ride (Toronto Transit Commission, The Toronto Public Transit, including buses, streetcars, and subways). As of August 2016, a TTC token is worth $3 within the city of Toronto, without a Metro pass. If your Uberpool trip is surged, or longer than a trip that usually costs $6, you still pay $6 for the trip.

For farther areas, outside of the downtown core, Uber applies a flat fare as estimated and based on suggested mileage and time. That means riders pay exactly the amount that the app estimates for the trip, no matter what the suggested direction or how much time the trip takes. It is a great saving for riders, but the drivers find it much harder.

In the United States of America, starting in September 2016, Uber is experimenting with a new flat rate of $2 to catch an UberPool in 6 cities: San Francisco, Seattle, Boston, Washington D.C., Miami and San Diego. Uber still keeps the option for your private ride, which is an UberX and will cost a flat rate of $7. The new $2 flat rate program is called UberPlus. To get the deal, a rider must first pay $20 for a month of up to 20 fixed-cost trips, or $30 for up to 40 trips. You'll be charged the flat rate in addition to the monthly fee.

"We're always thinking about ways to make Uber an affordable, everyday option, and this is a small beta we're running as part of that effort," Uber said in a statement.

Uber promises to pay the cut for drivers to top up their earnings as a normal UberPool fare. That means Uber drivers still earn the same UberPool fare as before. Uber realizes that the UberPool earning subsidy is still not enough for the driver partners (since UberPool is up to 40% cheaper than UberX and other platforms), so they sometimes adjust the fare during heavy traffic to compensate for the lost time (this does not change on rider fare). Uber also tops up extra money for any drivers who accept more UberPool trips per week, accordingly. Through the affordable UberPool idea, we can conclude that Uber has done the best for riders from low-income families, and tries their best to secure earnings for driver partners.

6.7.c Uber drivers' Vehicle Safety Checks:

In Toronto, as up to the new regulation, the city has assigned specific third parties, such as Canadian Tire, to have Uber drivers' vehicles safety checked. To encourage and make sure all partners follow the city rules, Uber has paid for drivers to have their cars safely checked at the designated autoshops for the first month from the effective date. A number of drivers have taken this advantage to save up to $80. In addition to implementing the city's new rules, Uber managed to work with First Advantage Canada to have all Uber drivers' backgrounds checked, without any fee being charged to Uber drivers.

6.7.d Connected trips:

Uber had learned and recognized that waiting time is a concern to their drivers. Uber drivers don't get paid for the waiting time. In downtown, during busy hours, there may be no waiting time, or a waiting time of only a few minutes. However, in suburb areas, or during slow times, the waiting time could go up to a couple of hours, depending on how many drivers are available, and in which areas. Some drivers complain more and more that new drivers getting on board create dead time, or make waiting times longer. In order to limit the waiting time, Uber's engineer team has updated the app with "connecting next trip." For connected trips, Uber drivers receive the next request right at the time when they are approaching the destination of the current drop-off. They go to pick up the next rider right off the bat. On Uber drivers' social media forum (fb.com/groups/UberToronto), the experienced drivers advise their fellow-partners to take the connecting trips wisely, based on time and location. In the downtown during rush hour, the connecting trips may take away your high surged trips. However, Uber's purpose of continuously connecting trips is pretty clear: to kill the waiting time for their drivers.

6.7.e "Go home" or "Set your destination":

Uber drivers used to waste an average of 70 minutes and 50 kilometres on driving from home to busy areas like the downtown core, and back again without any passenger in the back seat at the end of the day. Driver partners found it wasteful and wished that Uber could do something about it. Many driver partners, for a long time, had asked Uber to add a "Go Home" option. Finally, in the summer of 2016, the Uber Support Team answered driver partners' inquiries by rolling out the miraculous option called "Set Your Destination." This is even greater than the drivers' wish for a"Go Home" option. Two times, every day, Uber drivers can set their own destination. Uber wants their partners to use it appropriately, and not to abuse the function. Uber has a limit of two times for "Set your destination"– one at the beginning of the day to start driving, and the other one to go home when drivers finish for the day. They also limit matching time. If the Uber app has been searching the matched trips for more than a certain time (average 45 minutes, varies in cities), they will stop searching for the matched trips in the same directions. As a result, that Uber driver will lose one time of "Set your destination." In spite of the fact that some driver partners want more than the two times that are allowed for the setting, to take the best advantage of it (a number of Uber drivers work multiple periods of the day, not just once to work or once to go home), this addition has shown clear concrete support for their driver partners. It helps to add up to $100 per day for driver partners, and reduce the pollution from idling on the way to work and back home (average 50kms of idling). It is good for the environment.

6.7.f Good comments matter:

Besides financial support for a number of driver partners, Uber also finds various ways to reach out to their partners to see if there is anything that they can help non-financially. They might need motivation or mental support. Uber keeps sending out informative and supportive messages to notify their driver partners about upcoming events, holidays, or bad weather, so that they can prepare to work safely on these days. It is also a good time to double their earnings. Uber always advises their driver partners to keep it professional and take good care on the roads. Every week, Uber picks the best comments that riders have left after their trips, to compliment and motivate their drivers. The riders' good comments matter. Furthermore, Uber also has some good recommendations so that drivers can maintain high ratings. Next time, if you, as an Uber rider, enjoy your ride, don't forget to leave a positive comment, along with five stars. Uber will forward it to your driver. It will be shown as an anonymous, complimentary comment, but will help to shape the driver's behavior and improve professional service.

6.7.g Referrals:

Uber is a new rideshare business model. Their employment turnover is strangely high. They actually keep advertising and recruiting new drivers to join their partnership and workforce. It is said that they have been spending millions of dollars just on recruiting, every single day, across the cities, around the world. We have learned about the "newbies" and "dummies." Though there is a difference in earnings, the gap of knowledge and learning is what matters. Sooner or later, these drivers will realize that they have done it wrong and have to change. Their transformation puts the demand back to high again, and Uber has to step in and do the calculation in a timely manner. They have to bring on board enough forces to successively balance the demand to avoid surge pricing. As part of the recruitment, Uber shares their funding to their driver partners if they refer their friends or family to sign up and drive. Uber pays any driver a referral incentive that is worth anywhere from $100 to $250 (varies in cities) if the referred friend has completed a specific amount of required trips. For some driver partners, the referral does top up their income, but, in the long run, they are worried that it will hurt them. When the service supply is surplus, it may take the surge away and causes dead time. As we learned from the media in the past years, there are some drivers taking advantage of this referral promotion to earn as much as a medium annual salary, with barely having to drive.

6.7.h Fighting the citing of tickets:

Uber is recklessly fighting the legal battles somewhere around the world. Uber, a new business idea with technology advance, has been brutal controversy among the governments' authority officers and councillors. Many of them support rideshare, while others are against the operation. In some cities, councillors, who are against Uber, have ordered the police officers to ticket Uber drivers. These government members do that because they have different political opinions or maybe they have connections with the taxi monopoly to represent them in office. However, Uber is a strong and humble organization with one of the best legal teams in North America. They keep fighting till the end. They are willing to fight for their drivers' tickets. They even promise to pay for their drivers' tickets. Uber has said that they will back their drivers in legal battles. This makes their driver partners feel protected and stay strong together. The cited tickets are not cheap. They could be more than $500. With their continuous fighting strategy, and passion for innovation, Uber has been recognized and legalized to operate their rideshare business in many cities, including Toronto, Canada. The cities have finally realized that their people want various transportation choices for their daily commute, especially considering the new rideshare's convenience and affordability.

6.7.i Insurance coverage:

Uber is one of the fastest growing start-up businesses in the era of technology and science. They have successfully proved to the investors and to the people that their incorporation has multi-billion valuations. They have hundreds of thousands of driver partners around the world. With the job conditions, insurance coverage is the benefit that Uber driver partners care about the most. However, an insurance coverage solution for all partners isn't an easy problem to solve. A single miscalculation can cost the company billions of dollars in a second. Nonetheless, as we have witnessed, Uber has successively worked with automobile insurance companies to address the issue and get all their driver partners essentially insured, on the roads, as regulated. In Toronto, Uber has successfully worked with Intact Insurance Company to get commercial rideshare insurance coverage for all their Torontonian driver partners, in a timely fashion, on June 1, 2016.

6.7.j Job description and its leisure:

Uber has created one of the most interesting driving jobs in the market of modernized and casual life. Driver partners enjoy its flexibility, people networking, city sightseeing, and easy earning.

Flexibility: Driving for Uber is one of the most flexible jobs. Driver partners can log in (stay online) to drive, and log off anytime. They can drive any amount of time they need to. They can go *online* for 15 minutes, an hour, or 24 hours a day. They also can choose to drive one day a week, or seven days a week. There is no obligation to the time they have to spend on Uber platforms. If drivers want to take a vacation for a long time, even for more than two months, they can do that! They are advised to notify Uber staff so that their account will be kept safely on hold for when they return home and are able to work again.

Networking: Uber drivers have the chance to meet and talk to a lot of people from many classes in society. Uber riders may be pilots, engineers, doctors, scientists, photographers, etc. They learn a lot of things from personal stories and success stories. For drivers with English as their second language, they have a lot of chances to practice. They may be lucky enough to meet and talk to someone in their potential career field, and change their life.

No discrimination, and easier earnings – every time we step in an Uber, we see a different driver, from a different background. They are from different countries and can speak different languages. The only requirement is they have to pass the criminal and background check. Many Uber drivers are struggling to find a career. Driving for Uber helps them to get through financial difficulty while waiting for a real job offer. Surge pricing fares help to top up Uber drivers' earnings and encourage them to stick with the job longer. Through the app and technology, Uber transmits sufficient information so that their driver partners are able to have a pleasant customer service experience.

City sightseeing: Driving for Uber helps drivers discover the liveliest parts of the city. Even though Uber drivers can choose a specifically recommended location in which to drive, riders may take them anywhere within the city. Some even take long trips to neighboring cities. They will go to every corner, of any street, and any block. In fact, Uber drivers are potentially the greatest tour guides since they learn about so many sightseeing places, day by day.

Running a rideshare business model does not only require a top experienced and knowledgeable engineering team, but also a broad business vision toward consumers, employment, contractors or partnerships, third parties, and legal hallways. During the first half of 2016, Uber has taken care of their rider and driver partners more than in the past five years. As a result, Uber reported a 1.27 billion dollar loss for the first half of 2016 (see the chart on: fb.com/UberBook.KevinLy). Uber claims that topping up partners' earnings, and subsidies for UberPool's cheap rides, are the reasons for the downturn. As we can see, it is absolutely not easy for Uber to keep every party happy as they have done so far.

Chapter 7: UBER & THE LEGALIZATION CHALLENGE

Uber is one of the leading innovative technology companies from Silicon Valley. It is also known as one of the fastest growing tech-related start-up businesses. However, the adventures and victories of Uber have not always gone smoothly. Uber has gone through so many obstacles from competitors, partnerships, and legal issues. The difference in political beliefs and personalities of mayors and city councillors really matter in deciding whether to approve the legalization of rideshare companies, or not.

7.1 Toronto – Canada:

UBER first launched the rideshare service in March 2012. In the meantime, there hadn't been any clear municipal rules or provincial legislation for the new rideshare introduction. Despite the fact that Uber drivers were threatened by opposite authorities and the taxi monopoly, the Uber Toronto service has firmly kept the rideshare service running under Torontonians' love and solid support. During the challenging years between 2014 and early 2016, Uber Toronto has gone through several heated controversial debates in the City Hall.

On May 3, 2016, Toronto Mayor, John Tory, and City Council, voted to embrace the rideshare service.

On June 18, 2016, Uber claimed one trip in Toronto as one of the 147 trips around the world, celebrating what was the 2 billionth trip.

On July 7, 2016, Uber announced good news for Ontario; they have a new ridesharing policy from Intact Insurance & Assurance Company, designed especially for riders and driver partners.

On August 16, 2016, The City of Toronto granted a PTC (Private Transportation Company) license to Uber. Uber is officially legalized to operate in Toronto. Uber has won a big victory in Canada.

7.2 London – United Kingdom:

On June 11, 2014, *black cab* drivers disrupted traffic as a protest against Transport for London's refusal to stop Uber.

On October 16, 2015, Transport for London brought a case to the high court. They ruled that the Uber app is legal in London.

7.3 Philippines:

On October 23, 2014, the Philippine Land Transportation Franchising and Regulatory Board (LTFRB) set fines on Uber drivers. However, Uber was endorsed by the Metropolitan Manila Development Authority.

On October 30, 2014, an intervention from the Department of Transportation and Communications made the LTFRB suspend its ban on Uber.

On May 10, 2015, the country's Department of Transportation and Communications granted Uber a new classification as The Transportation Network Vehicle Service. Uber was legalized to operate with a required GPS installation.

7.4 New Zealand:

In January 2015, Uber faced difficulty with the Land Transport Act, with fines of up to NZ$10,000.

On January 20, 2015, Craig Foss, the Associate Transport Minister, said his government would review the Uber rideshare service by mid 2015.

In April and May 2016, Uber drivers were threatened by the New Zealand Transport Authority (NZTA) and were issued warnings.

7.5 Amsterdam – The Netherlands:

On December 8, 2014, Dutch judges banned UberPop.

Uber responded to The Hague-based Trade and Industry Appeals Tribunal ruling by indicating that the company would continue to offer the service, despite the €100,000 fine and the €40,000 fine for their drivers.

7.6 New Delhi – India:

In December 2014, Uber was banned from New Delhi for not following the city's compulsory police verification procedure.

Almost 7,000 people signed a petition calling on Uber to conduct mandatory seven-year background checks on drivers. Uber said it would work with the Indian government "to establish clear background checks currently absent in their commercial transportation licensing programs."

As of March 2016, Uber is still operating in New Delhi.

7.7 Hong Kong:

On August 11, 2015, Hong Kong Police raided Uber's office after arresting Uber drivers.

On its website, the Hong Kong government investment agency, InvestHK, had been endorsing Uber as one of its *success stories.* It has been removed since Uber cannot meet the legal requirements in Hong Kong.

7.8 Brussels – Belgium:

From March to June 2014, Uber was threatened with having to pay a €10,000 (US $13,500) fine, if drivers got pulled over. The city required a taxi license.

In June 2014, Uber advertised for a Brussels-based *General Manager,* on the *LinkedIn* website.

In 2014, Brussels Mobility minister, Pascal Smet, announced that the city authorities planned to create a legal framework by 2016 to allow the consideration of the new rideshare service in the city.

In 2016, Uber operates UberX and UberBlack services in Brussels. By taking an Uber ride in Belgium, you agree to become a member of the *Platform Rider Association.*

7.9 Rio de Janeiro – Brazil:

On April 29, 2015, a Brazilian court banned Uber in response to complaints by a taxi drivers' union. A few weeks later, the order was revoked. They allowed Uber to operate normally although still in a legal debate in São Paulo and Rio de Janeiro.

In October 2015, the mayor of São Paulo, Fernando Haddad, passed a bill to allow Uber to operate.

7.10 China:

As we know, China is the toughest market for American companies to enter. Most Sillicon Valley tech giants such as Uber, Facebook, Google, and Amazon, failed in China. The reason is because China is worried about censorship and IP theft. Chinese government regulations favour domestic champions. China is Uber's largest market (more than a third of its business) based on weekly ride reports.

In February 2014, Uber has a formal launch in China with luxury car services in three Chinese cities: Shanghai, Guangzhou and Shenzhen.

In December 2014, Chongqing police raided a training session, involving more than 20 Uber drivers.

In April 2015, Chinese authorities raided the offices of Uber in Guangzhou, Guangdong.

On May 6, 2015, local police raided the offices of Uber in Chengdu, in Sichuan province.

Uber losses are more than one billion dollars as Uber fights for market share against its powerful Chinese rival, Didi.

In 2015, Kalanick spent five days in China in a *hands-on* role as chief executive of Uber China.

In September 2015:, Uber China raised one billion dollars from investors.

In 2015, Didi raised more than two billion dollars from investors, including Tencent, Alibaba, and China's sovereign wealth fund, CIC.

In 2016, Didi became the largest ride-sharing group in the country. Didi has operations in more than 400 cities in China. It has just closed a fresh funding round of four and a half billion dollars from investors, including Apple.

Didi and Uber have entered the toughest battle to become the number one rideshare service in China. A number of Didi customers are switching to Uber since Uber rides are much cheaper.

7. 11 Copenhagen – Denmark:

In November 2014, The National Transport Authority filed a police complaint after Uber Black and UberPop was launched in Copenhagen.

In January 2015, Denmark's transport minister, who was not opposed to Uber, said the app was "contrary" to Danish law in terms of consumer safety and employee training.

On July 8, 2016, Danish police charged more than 48 Uber drivers for "offering taxi services without license."

7.12 Paris – France:

(Paris is the unfriendliest market for Uber.)

In early 2014, Uber launched UberPop, in Paris. DGCCRF (The Directorate-General for Competition, Consumer Affairs and Product Quality/Safety) began to consider banning UberPOP.

October 17, 2014, the court stated that UberPop violated a pre-existent regulation that bans carpooling for profit, and fined Uber €100,000 (US $128,000) for "deceptive practice."

In mid November 2014, Uber launched UberPool to replace UberPop. At the time, Pierre-Dimitri Gore-Coty was Uber's Western Europe chief.

On December 12, 2014, a French court ruled that Uber could face a $25,000 fine, if advertising.

On January 1, 2015, UberPop service was banned in Paris.

As of February 23, 2015, about 100 drivers, mostly first-time offenders, had been ticketed.

In June 2015, French authorities arrested Uber managers, Thibault Simphal, and Pierre-Dimitri Gore-Coty, on six charges, including "deceptive commercial practices, complicity in instigating an illegal taxi-driving activity, and the illegal stocking of personal information." Meanwhile, taxi drivers carried out the most aggressively violent protest against Uber.

In June 2016, a Paris court fined Uber €800,000 for "illegally" running its Uberpop service in 2015.

7.13 Berlin & Frankurt – Germany:

In April 2014, Berlin ruled against Uber in a case filed by the Berlin Taxi Association.

On August 13, 2014, the city banned the service from operating in Berlin. Uber faced a €25,000 (Euro) (US $33,400) fine.

On March 18, 2015, the Frankfurt district court banned UberPop.

In May 2015, Uber ceased UberPop and replaced it with UberX (which is now compatible with German law, similar to a conventional chauffeur service).

7.14 Other cities:

Read about the other cities here: www.fb.com/UberBook.KevinLy

This chapter has shown the marvelous steps that Uber has gone through around the world. We really appreciate that Uber has successfully brought the convenient and reliable rideshare service to our city. For those in the cities that Uber is still fighting for, we wish them all good luck; hopefully their governments and leaders will take quick steps to accommodate the economic service so that people can go with the trend and have a choice.

Link to sources: www.fb.com/UberBook.KevinLy

Chapter 8: UBER DRIVER/RIDER MUTUAL RESPECT

Misunderstanding is fundamentally caused from invisibility and misperception. It sometimes causes frustration among Uber riders and drivers. Here are some recommendations that help to find solutions so that Uber partners and customers can build good relationships, have mutual respect, and have fun during their daily rides. These also improve communication, and create smooth pickups.

8.1 What do riders need to know when ordering an Uber?

8.1.a What is the best practice for an accurate pickup?
As we all know, we have two ways to order an Uber to come to pick us up through the Uber App:

Method 1: Riders enter the actual address of their current location where they want the driver to come to pick them up. This method is correct and recommended by Uber.

Method 2: Riders drop the ping around the pickup location or just turn on GPS (GPS locates exactly where you are). This method is being used by busy, lazy, or drunk people who think it takes hours to enter their address. Dropping the ping is sometimes not 100% accurate since the

Uber map is minimized down to a smartphone screen size. This means that with just a slight touch of your finger, by accident, can move the ping blocks away from your neighborhood. When you are drunk, chances are that you will get charged a $5.00 cancellation fee because you moved the ping out of your city. Your driver arrives and has no clue where you are. This mistake also happens to first time riders. To make it beneficial, always double check the address, and whether it matches with yours or not.

The best way to have your driver pick you up at the exact spot where you are standing: In many busy cities, the address is not as easy to find as we think – there may be some missing numbers; the street numbers may be too small or have faded away; street numbers can't be seen on some high buildings; it is too hard to see a clear number on business buildings, on busy streets, like in the downtown. That's why, even when you enter an exact address, your driver can still struggle with finding where you are. How about making all street numbers a giant size? Sure, that is great, and maybe will be someone's upcoming business idea. However, there is a better way for it. If you are living or working in an office located on a busy street or in a complicated plaza, you had better enter your company name, a store, a restaurant nearby, or, wherever you can meet your driver more easily (i.e. LYSON MEDIA Inc, 100 King Street West, Toronto). Indicating a popular pizza store, or a coffee shop, could help. In this way, even if your driver can't see the street number, he or she can identify the pickup place (LYSON MEDIA Inc.) promptly. The other way that you can make it easier is to add the nearest intersection. Unlike drivers having difficulty in finding an address, most drivers are able to recognize the location quickly if we tell them the intersection.

8.1.b Ideal pickup point:

As a customer (rider), we all want to take advantage of the convenience of Uber. We want our Uber driver to stop their car right in front of our doorstep. However, we don't see the hassles that drivers have to face with the ongoing traffic during rush hours, especially in the downtown where most commuters don't own a car. They may not have caught up with new restrictions and traffic signs that the city keeps applying time to time. Next time, before you order an Uber, remember to check if your pickup location is a sensitive spot or not:

The street where your apartment is located has a bike lane. That means that no emergency stops are allowed. Some drivers may stick around illegally to wait for you. We know they are unhappy and nervous at the moment. If they get caught, they will be fined at least $500 (varies in cities). In spite of the fact that Uber has a five-minute waiting policy, drivers find it really long and get frustrated in this situation. In rush hour, when the traffic keeps moving, there is no chance for drivers to stop, even for a few seconds. The driver will be stressed out by the honking horns of impatient drivers. In this case, you had better drop the ping in a nearby alleyway, or in a spacious public parking lot where your driver can wait for you without any hassles. By doing that, it may require you to walk to the recommended pickup spot. Sometimes, we need to walk a block away to an ideal pickup location. Nonetheless, the less traffic there is, the easier it is for a pickup.

For example, if you try to order an Uber from an annual festival spot where thousands of participants are going, chances are that you will have to walk out of the crowd to be visible to your driver, since your driver has no access to a festival fleet. Even if they can find access into the festival, both you and your driver will have a hard time finding each other in the crowd. It is also a peak time of Uber business; so all drivers are in hurry. Again, chances are that you will get charged a $5.00 cancellation fee, if you are too lazy.

Similarly, ordering Uber from a provincial park or a zoo causes difficulties in picking up. These places are located on a huge section of land. If you use ping, chances are that the ping will be dropped in the middle of nowhere in the park or zoo. It will take you some time to make a call and explain where you are. Instead, you had better look around to find a good spot. Maybe walk out to the gate and see what the street name and number are. If there were a store or a business there, it would be much better. Then that would be the ideal spot to drop the ping or enter the address.

8.1.c Tipping:

This topic has been discussed in chapter two. From the beginning, Uber has urged their customers (passengers/riders) not to tip their servers (Uber drivers) by the use of tricky language: "Experience cashless" or "Everything is included, no need to tip." Uber does this because they want everyone to be able to afford to take an Uber. Tipping used to be a sensitive conversation during Uber trips, until the middle of the year 2016. Uber drivers were discouraged to hang a tipping sign in their vehicles due to rating affects and deactivation threats. If you are a well-educated individual, you would quickly realize that Uber drivers are those who are working in the service sector, and tipping is definitely encouraged and appreciated whenever or wherever possible. We don't need to tip every single day when we go to work. However, it is an absolute courtesy to tip our Uber driver during good occasions (i.e. Read Chapter 2). It has never been said, but when you take an Uber at a high surged time, the tip is literally included. Either way, it brings happiness and excitement to the driver. Moreover, tipping helps to identify and separate you from the crowd. For Uber drivers, when you tip them, they would look at you differently since they rarely get tipped. They would think you are a well-educated person. You understand the sector. Your kindness is visible. You are a *real* human being. You are from a middle class family or above. If you are spotted, well dressed and tipping, you become the top 1% high-class, in their eyes. That's fantastic, isn't it? Nowadays, people do judge a book by its cover. That's why we dress to succeed, and behave properly.

If you are from a low-income family, you are still welcome on routes by drivers and Uber. Uber drivers do have morals. They don't insist on being tipped from everybody. Most of them are from low-income families. When they don't drive, they do need to take Uber sometimes. So, they totally understand and empathize with those who are struggling with financial problems. In this case, after getting to your destination safely, you can give your driver five stars and leave a complimentary and supportive comment so that Uber recognizes their driver's accomplishment. For sure, your Uber driver finds it mentally healing. It is greater than the tipping of a few bucks.

8.1.d Be aware of a $200 fee for puking or making a mess in Uber cars:

Not all Uber riders have known that Uber will investigate and charge a "cleaning" fee of up to $200 on top of no matter how long or short the trip was, if they find out the rider left a mess in their driver's car. Uber applies this fee to compensate their driver for earning time lost. Imagine, on a weekend night, the driver just starts his ten-hour driving schedule. After a drinking party, you or your friend, as riders, hop in and puke in his car, which stops your driver from driving and earning on that otherwise good night. Your driver has to wait until the following morning when the service opens to clean the mess. He or she could have made at least $200 throughout the night. That charge is quite expensive for your short trip, but reasonable for the service.

You may not intentionally cause the incident, but it is totally avoidable. You know what you and your close friends' drinking tolerance is, so make sure you prepare for it. When you take Uber with your kids, and bring food or drink on board, make sure you ask for the driver's permission. You eat and drink carefully in the back seats. Try keeping the spillable liquids closed up tightly. You had better have it well wrapped and covered.

8.1.e Should Uber riders eat or drink in Uber cars?
On a busy day, we may not have enough time to have a breakfast. We just wrap a sandwich and eat on the run. Some women put on their makeup in Uber cars too. We all know it saves time. However, eating in your own car and in a service vehicle is not the same.

For your own car: people have different personalities. Some people are super clean. They always keep their car smelling good, and looking tidy. They probably never allow anyone to eat in their car. They, themselves, of course, never bring food or drink in their car. These types of people always politely ask for an Uber driver's permission if they want to eat in their car. On the other hand, some people don't really care and never have their car cleaned or washed. Eating on the run is something they consider normal. This type of rider usually does not ask for the driver's permission. They just eat. They think if they pay for the ride, eating or drinking is their right.

What do Uber drivers really think when you eat in their cars? Again, Uber drivers fall into two categories: the *clean* type and the *nasty* type. That means some drivers will let you eat in their cars, on the run; yet some other drivers will remind you. In a survey in the social media forum, over 90% of Uber drivers are not pleasant at all if their riders bring food and eat in their clean cars, especially the hot food with strong smells (the survey on: fb.com/groups/UberToronto). Why? When we are hungry, the fresh, hot food makes us feel like we are starving. We want to eat. However, when the food is stored, or kept for hours, the smell turns disgustingly stronger. The other reason is that people like or dislike different tastes or flavors. For instance, some people like durian; but for a lot of people, they think durian has a stinky smell. Part of the world likes cooking and eating curry, but some people don't like it when someone brings this smell near them. An Uber driver gives rides to hundreds of different customers a week. All passengers are not the same. You leave your terrific food smells that you think of as being ok, but the next rider steps in and has no clue where the smell is coming from. Chances are that they may judge that the smell is from the driver; for sure, it is a totally awkward and unpleasant trip that you don't want to take for hours. So next time, you probably should think twice whether you really need to eat in Uber cars. If you are a busy type of person, and have no other time to eat, make sure you ask for the Uber driver's permission to eat in his or her car. It helps to maintain your high rating, and respect your Uber driver.

8.1.f Should the riders bring animals, such as cats or dogs?

You are animal-friendly. You have been raising a dog or a cat to amuse yourself. Sometimes you need to take your pet out for a health check. You are treating your pet like a baby that needs your attention. So, you take them to work or a daycare. Or, you merely take them out with you for fun. Sure, you have a thousand of reasons to take your pet out, and you decide to take an Uber. There are different types of Uber drivers, and ones who are also animal-friendly. They don't mind when you bring your pet along. The other types of Uber drivers may or may not be animal-friendly, but it matters if an animal is brought in their car. They just don't like your pet to make a mess in their service car. They may worry for the next riders who are allergic to animals (maybe the hair or smell). They have a new car, so they don't want your pet hair in the back seat. Sometimes, they joke by asking if your pet has been given a bath or a shower. But they already know for sure that if they allow your pet on board, the pet will leave some hair or a strong smell in the car. Uber allows their drivers to accept or refuse a ride with animals, except for service animals (by law). Since it matters, you should call your Uber driver ahead of time to confirm if he or she will allow your pet on the trip. It helps to maintain your rating and avoid being charged a $5.00 cancellation fee.

8.1.g Riders pay for the ride, so do they have a right to make any stops on the way?

Sure, you can ask your driver to stop anywhere you want. You have that right. You think this because you are willing to pay for the running meter. In reality, this is something that should never be done during a trip. Uber and taxi are two different business models: cab service and rideshare. The reason why the rideshare model was born, was to compete with the taxi pricing. In order to have a more affordable fare, the rideshare reduces the price, or charges less, here and there. You may, or may not, know that Uber drivers are paid an average of $0.18 (18 cents) per minute in timing (a typical taxi used to be $4 per minute). For example: if you have to stop by somewhere during a trip for 30 minutes. That means the Uber driver earns 0.18x30 = $5.40 in that half an hour of waiting for you. Basically, in this case, your Uber driver earns less than a minimum wage. A net fare that an Uber driver earns is based on a minimum, or base fare, plus time per minute, plus mileage, after the Uber commission. In a standard market, like the city of Toronto, where a trip is merely on a highway with an average speed of 100 kilometres per hour, an Uber driver could earn an average $60 per hour. With the same distance of traveling, the less time Uber drivers spend on roads, the higher the value of the fare is. Therefore, picking the routes, pausing the trip, making the driver wait, or long pickups, are the factors that directly affect the value of the fare. As a rider, if you have financial freedom, and are trying to treat your Uber driver well, you are believed to have the best and easiest solution. For all others, if you must make a stop somewhere during the Uber trip, perhaps for a burger or to get a coffee through the drive thru, make sure it does not exceed five minutes. Otherwise, you had better end the trip and make a second request after you are done with your stop. We all know that it takes an average of five minutes for a driver to come to pick us up. Exceptionally, if it is a high surge priced trip, the driver doesn't mind waiting for you because the surge pricing partly covers the "dead" time. Ultimately, you will feel good when you make others happy. You look bad when you do something wrong to people, and later they complain about you (like on social media) behind your back. Understanding the driver's income would help you use Uber moderately and rationally.

8.1.h When to use an UberPool:

Everyone is welcome and advised to use UberPool to reduce traffic jams and pollution. UberPool is a great *product* from Uber that aligns with the city in climate change and traffic infrastructure solutions. Taking UberPool makes you a part of the *Green* activity. However, we need to know when it is the right time to take UberPool. All these riders who have taken UberPool are aware of this experience. You have 30 minutes to get to the airport for check-in in a timely manner. If you decide to take an UberPool, you may end up missing your flight. Your Uber driver is supposed to pick up any Poolmates on the way to the airport, as much as four riders at a time. When the driver drops one off, they need to pick one up. After the driver drops two, they may pick up another two...until the Uber car is fully packed. It is an endless trip, and your stop (airport) is just one of many stops on an UberPool trip. It is the same direction to the airport, but it doesn't mean in a straight line. It may go south a bit, then back north a bit. Sometimes, it goes backwards to catch the other riders. As a result, UberPool takes a lot more time compared to UberX. With UberX, it takes you approximately 30 minutes to get to the airport. However, UberPool may take two full hours to get to the destination. If your time is tight, or you have to show up at an event on time, UberPool is NOT recommended for you. If you have a lot of time, or are on a tour around the city, or you like meeting new people and networking, you are welcome to take UberPool. The other main purpose that Uber rolls out UberPool is to keep the rides more affordable for low-income families. Though it is less convenient than other Uber platforms, UberPool helps to make taking an Uber real and affordable for everyone.

The other thing about UberPool that we need to take into account is that Uber drivers earn 40% less from UberPool than UberX, or others. UberX drivers support the idea that UberPool helps to fight climate change and go *green* with the environment, but it is really interrupting their income. It is a pain. Uber does have some incentive to top up the Pool trips, but still can't compete with the rate that drivers can earn from an UberX, or others. For those who insist in taking UberPool at the right time, and tip their drivers for the lost earnings, they are good role models of rideshare pioneers.

8.1.i Your drivers are literally computerized through the app and technology:
Why a rider thinks ordering an Uber is very simple: open app, punch in the location, wait for about five to ten minutes, driver comes and picks them up at their doorstep. However, those who are operating

the vehicles need to observe outside and inside. Uber drivers have to follow each step, guided by the computer and application system. They also face the city's traffic complex (No left/right turn, one way, No U-turn...). Drivers can only see less than 70% outside (varies on conditions), so they have to drive and look around carefully. At the same time, they need to take a quick look at the directions, address number and street name, passenger names, etc. Sometimes the app doesn't work properly. The location and the ping are slightly different, and drivers have to double check to make sure they are picking up the right rider. That's why they are advised to always ask their rider their name before starting the trip. As a rider, be patient and give drivers some time to do the job.

8.1.j How to rate your Uber driver:

The rating system of Uber is working efficiently in a five star scale. Uber suggests drivers rate their passengers with five stars if everything is going well, and two stars if there are serious problems like racism, harassment, aggressive language, or violence. In fact, most Uber drivers go ahead and give passengers five stars as a process to quickly end a trip. They only take a few extra minutes to think about rating the rider when something goes wrong on route. In The United State of America, a number of drivers take rating the passengers seriously. Some drivers set a standard rating chart for themselves. For example, if a rider doesn't tip them, they would give four, instead of five, stars. A lot of factors are brought in to consider the decision. In Canada, Uber drivers are a little easier with the rating. Even a normal ride (not super cool, no tip), chances are that you will still get five stars from your driver. Of course, tipping may secure your five star rating. If the rider has taken Uber for a while, and has a bad rating, Uber drivers will look at them differently. They think something is wrong with them. They would advise their fellow drivers to carefully accept the low-rated passengers. In their experience, those with bad ratings would not treat their drivers fairly through their language and behavior. The rating matters to riders, as well as to Uber drivers. Uber used to be extremely strict on their partners. A driver with a bad rating would be given a notice or warning. If not improved, that driver would be deactivated or permanently logged out of the Uber platform. In order to get back on track, that Uber driver would have to pay for, and pass, an education course or improvement class, conducted by a third party. Some passengers do not rate their rides at all. Many other riders do rate their rides. That means they care about the service.

But are the riders using it precisely? Here are some types of riders rating Uber drivers:

Type1: (Typical riders) These riders just apply one frequent typical rating to almost every Uber driver they meet (**three stars** for all drivers), except for a few "super cool" or "good looking" drivers. It's their habit.

Type2: (Happy riders) The way they rate their Uber drivers is exactly the same as the way most of drivers rate their passengers. Typically, they just give out **five stars** for anyone after the trip ends. They are nice!

Type 3: (The judges) These are people who judge a book by its cover. They give their driver five stars if they like him/her, and a low rating for those that they dislike or hate. Uber drivers claim this type is "the racist."

Type 4: (High-class mind) These riders believe the rating on Uber is working exactly the same as the one applied in hotels, restaurants or resorts. Whoever gets five stars must be offering an outstanding, luxurious, professional, and extraordinary service.

Type 5: (Rational riders) These riders are well educated, professional and *rational*. They know the first day Uber came to their city. They appreciate the convenient service and technology. They know how to make themselves and others happy. The most important thing for them is their driver taking them to their destination safely, and on the best mutually agreed route. They know how the rating system affects driver partners. They know that a smile, high rating, and complimentary comments will motivate and shape Uber drivers at the end of the day. Through friendly conversation, they know how to help drivers understand what is important in the rating decision. Ultimately, they still keep giving out five stars to show their continuous support for the rideshare and technology.

8.2 Driver Toward Rider:

Uber is one of the smartest business models in the world. It applies the most advanced technology. However, it is also the most complicated enterprise to deal with in regard to customer service. It is hard to make everybody happy. Uber, driver partners, and riders are three different parties in this business. It is a headache for Uber to figure out how to grow a smooth business while still keeping outstanding customer service, and making sure that drivers make enough money to cover all driving expenses and costs. We have learned how the riders should treat their drivers. In the second part of this chapter, we will help driver partners to shape their profession:

8.2.a Know who you are picking up:

Everyone drives for Uber for different purposes. Not all drivers make the same money. Some drivers join in the rideshare system and just work part time. Some former taxi drivers apply exactly the same way they did at a taxi company to Uber platforms. Some entrepreneurs learn the surge pricing and come to make the most out of it. Driving sounds like a very simple and easy job, but sometimes the frustration can go up to a maximum level. Drivers get stressed out for various reasons. It affects the way they welcome the passengers – sometimes negative, sometimes positive. In order to eliminate the negative issues, here are some facts that Uber drivers need to keep in mind to have a different outlook of the rideshare service:

When a rider steps in an Uber driver's car, the Uber driver has no idea who the rider is. The fact is that the rider may be an off-duty police officer. The rider may be a professor. The rider may be an engineer. The rider may be a doctor. The rider may be an undercover Uber staff member. The rider may be a first time rider or a tourist from some other city or state. Say, you are speeding unintentionally or are driving impaired, and you don't know that your passenger is an off-duty officer. Then you get into trouble. When you pick up a first time rider, you are representing Uber and all partners to make sure that the first time rider has a good experience on platforms so that they will tell their network positive things about this business. At the time, if your behavior is bad, they wouldn't take Uber again. Uber does not only lose one customer, but they lose that part of a network, and your job has more down time (dead time).

When you drive for Uber, it is just an occasional or part time job. You pick up the city's citizens and take them to work, or back home daily. However, when you pick up visitors, your role is more important than just a driver. You play a great role as an Uber representative, as a tourism ambassador, and as the face of your city. You are responsible for what you do. The visitors will appraise the hospitality of your city through you. It is your driving safety and customer service experience.

8.2.b Uber drivers need to apply the cancellation fee reasonably:
We all know Uber has applied a $5.00 cancellation fee policy in order to compensate for the time their driver partners lose when they come

to pick up riders but the riders do not show up, or cancel the trip. This fee is totally reasonable because Uber driver do not get paid for the time they wait, or come to pickup at a location. It may take your driver more than 10 minutes to come to pick you up (varies on locations and traffic conditions). Some Uber drivers are taking advantage of this policy to cancel riders, no matter what. They don't even call their riders after they arrive. They believe it is punishment for the rider so that the rider will learn from this experience, and had better be ready on time for the next ride. Uber has stepped in and reminded these drivers. It does affect their rating. The following analysis of reasons why the riders don't show up would help Uber drivers know when to cancel the trip and get the $5.00 cancellation fee. Here are some good reasons that drivers are advised to cancel the trip and move on during busy times:

Reason 1: The Uber driver has tried to call two times within five minutes, but neither one of the calls was answered. There was no sign that the rider would show up. In this case, Uber wants their drivers to move on since the demand may be high.

Reason 2: The Uber driver has called, and the rider answered the call, and told the driver to wait for more than 10 minutes more.

Reason 3: The rider tries to ping around other areas to avoid surge pricing, then calls the driver to come to the actual pickup. If the actual pickup location is too far (i.e. more than 500m, and the traffic moves very slow during rush hours. 500m may take another 10 minutes to get there), Uber offers a reason called "Wrong address" cancellation for Uber drivers to cancel on these riders. Uber literally tries to send a message to those riders: "Sorry, we are too busy, no time to play."

The other reasons that Uber drivers should never cancel, or think twice before cancelling:

Reason 1: The rider may be a first time rider. They need more time to get used to the Uber application to see how it works.

Reason 2: The rider has something suddenly come up (like finding keys, try to wrap something they forgot) and can't get ready in time. They call their Uber driver to wait for a couple more minutes. If the driver cancels the trip, the rider will be late for work or for an appointment.

Reason 3: Uber drivers may try to call, and understand if the riders are from low-income families. $5.00 means a lot for them, so waiting a few extra minutes for them would be worth it. If you insist in moving on, Uber has a good cancellation clause called "Do not charge the rider." Let human faith be restored.

8.2.c What should Uber drivers wear?
That is the most popular question that a new Uber driver would ask when they sign up to drive. Uber does not require their drivers to dress

up or wear a suit, or any specific thing. However, the way Uber drivers dress is important because it partly affects their rating. In particular, UberBlack drivers who serve mostly high-class businessmen or party people need to look professional. Dressing is based on the season too. During cool weather, Uber drivers had better dress up in casual business attire (suit, jacket, or tie is not necessary). They must look clean and professional because that way the riders trust and feel comfortable, and have an enjoyable ride. In the hot summer, drivers don't need to overdress, or wear long pants with a jacket. Though it is a hot summer day, drivers should always keep a fashionable look. A shower before work is recommended at all times. People have different tastes, so wearing too strong of a perfume is not a good idea.

8.2.d Is it okay if Uber drivers play loud music?

We all know there are some optimistic drivers who turn their music up loud. However, when they drive for Uber, listening to loud music could harm their rating since people are different. Some people just need an Uber ride. That is it. Furthermore, everyone at various ages does not listen to the same kind of music. The young teenagers like listening to the Top 40. Some middle-aged men like country music. The elderly can only listen to light music like jazz or classical music. Crazy people might be interested in rock. Some people have a specific taste for Indy music. When they listen to their favorite music, they enjoy it and feel excited. However, when they are forced to listen to another kind of music that they are not interested in, they feel annoyed and get a headache. They just want to shut it down or run away. Some people even say that they don't like music! They just want a peaceful atmosphere for thinking. Indeed, the first things the top Uber driver partners always ask for is riders' opinions: the riders' usual route, category of music, whether they like AC or prefer fresh air, etc. By asking, you will find out what they are really interested in and what they are not really keen on. Respecting your riders' choice, making them happy, and giving them complete peace of mind, could definitely enrich your customer service experience and boost your rating.

8.2.e Riders are either from 99% or 1%:

By cutting the fare to the lowest and creating alternative products and services, Uber has successfully encouraged millions of people to take Uber as daily commute choice. Uber service is no longer for the rich, but everyone can afford to take it whenever they need. The riders could be from a low-income family, to high-class businessmen or millionaires. We have all types of Uber platforms such as UberBike, UberMotobike, UberX, UberBlack, UberChopper, UberPrivateJet, and so on. In other words, Uber is for both the 99% and 1% class of society. UberX is the most popular platform, and people take millions of trips around the world, every single day. From the vision of Uber's CEO Travis Kalanick to the way Uber operates and manages, there is literally a clear message to UberX drivers: we have tried to make UberX more and more affordable for everyone to take, not just for the rich. In order to make it feasible, Uber has done a lot of improvement in market pricing and catering. The most common mistake that a number of UberX drivers make is that they think UberX riders (UBER customers) are rich! They assume that all riders should be nice enough to tip, especially those professional people who live downtown areas. In fact, there are a certain number of people who like living downtown; and others don't. Of course, living downtown costs a lot; not only rich people, but those young millennia, from low to middle class families, also find a way to survive in the most vibrating core area of the city. Generally speaking, Uber drivers only have a 1% chance to pick up the rich, and a 99% chance to pick up the general people. Rare tipping on UberX trips is clearly understandable. Or, working on surge pricing only gives Uber drivers a lot of time to wait. Basically, the 99% can't afford to take Uber when the service demand is far higher than the supply. Like many Uber drivers, most of the riders are still living on monthly pay cheques or wages. Understanding their city, and people, would help Uber drivers realize this, and behave better towards one another. We are all adults. It is our mature responsibility to keep human faith restored for all generations. Uber on!

Chapter 9: UBER & ROAD STORIES

According to Uber Toronto Driver Network (Uber Toronto Partners Forum: facebook.com/groups/UberToronto), driving for Uber is one of the most adventurous but also the most amusing jobs. Every single day, Uber drivers learn so many stories and lessons, intentionally and unintentionally. The stories are different: domestic violence issues, cheating, business insiders, crazy pickups, tears, and laughs. They occasionally pick up a stripper, a prostitute, a comedian, a superstar, a jerk, a creep, a dancer...

Here are some crazy and funny stories from Uber Partners forums:

9.1 Drivers' stories:

Driver story #1: *"Yesterday evening, I got a request and went to pick up a passenger in Liberty village. When I was arrived at the location, a middle-aged lady, appearing angry, showed up and jumped in my car without saying anything. I could guess that she just had a domestic problem or argument with her family. She rudely answered with a single inappropriate word every time I asked. "Mr, can you be more aggressive?" she complained. I wished I could have done better, but the heavy traffic didn't let me move faster. It was rush hour. She said, in a loud voice, "Why don't people move! ... it's a green light!" At the end of the trip, she hopped out and slammed the door without saying goodbye. That was the last trip of a long day for me. The woman made me feel that my Uber day was even longer and heavier. I ended the trip and ran away. On the way home, I sent the woman a message: "Dear Ma'am, I just kicked a tree for no reason. Now my ankle is swelling and is painful as hell. Thank you ma'am. You have succeeded in passing your stress on to me. Next time, please request an "UberAmbulance" instead, if you are in a rush. Thank you. Wish one of us had a good night."*

Driver story #2: "I picked up a lady at 100 King Street West in the evening. She just finished work and needed to run to a gala dinner. She was in a hurry. She didn't have time to change. She was still in her work uniform. When the car was running for 200ms, as usual, I looked back to check the traffic to avoid rear-end collisions. What I saw was that she had turned my back seat into her change room. She stripped down to almost nothing. Of course her underwear were still on. She was replacing her business casual with a sexy black skirt. I let the car run. It never happened before. My attention to the traffic was reduced down to 90% of my concentration. My creepy eye took the other 10% away, specifically for the disruptive movement in the back seat. The most ridiculous thing was that when she hopped out of my car, there was a quick strong wind that blew up her skirt. She was embarrassed because everybody around my car caught the moment. I thought the strip show was only for me. Man, it was the most dangerous ride ever!"

Driver's story #3: *"I picked up these two drunk girls at a bar and was about halfway to their house when the one girl asks how I like driving for Uber. I told her it's been good so far, and that I wish more people knew about the service. I said "Spread the word!" and the girl replied, half slurring her words, "I'll spread the word, then spread my legs ... Do you have a girlfriend?"*

I laughed pretty hard and informed her that I was married. Her friend apologized on her behalf and that was the end of that."

Driver's story #4: *"My good friend (a guy) picked up a couple of gay dudes from a party one night to drive them home. The passengers spent the entire ride trying to convince my friend to come with them to the bedroom for blowjobs, buggery, etc., which my friend politely declined. After the trip, the passenger gave him a one star review with the comment, 'sexual harassment.' My friend was kicked off of Uber and is no longer allowed to drive for them."*

Driver's story #5: *"A couple of weeks ago, I was heading home from my shift. It was 3 AM, Saturday morning, and I was about halfway home when I get a ping to pick someone up at IHOP. I figured that one more ride wouldn't hurt. I picked the guy up. Let's call him Steve.*

So, Steve gets in my car, apologizes for the 'long trip' we are about to have, and hands me a twenty dollar bill. I work in the Rockford area, in Illinois, and when I started the trip, his destination was in Kenosha, Wisconsin, 88 miles away. I knew it was going to be a long ride, but I figured I'd be making some decent money.

Here starts the trip, which would be three hours, round-trip. Ten minutes into the ride, this guy is passed out in my backseat, so I figured I'd just play some tunes and enjoy the quiet ride. Five more minutes go by, and suddenly he's sitting upright, looks at me, and proceeds to vomit all over my floor, the back of my seat, and on my door, as well as under the passenger seat. He hands me another twenty, and passes out again, while I've still got over an hour to get him home (3:20 AM at this point).

It's 40-Fahrenheit degrees (4C) outside, and I have to drive with all my windows down, on the highway, the whole way there. I ended up dropping him off after he vomited two more times, in the same spots on my floor. Then I had to make the hour and a half trip home, alone, and cold as fuck. I got back into town at 6 AM, had to wait till 8:30 AM for the cleaner to open, and wasn't home till nearly 11 AM.

Not too horrible, but definitely my worst night driving."

(The driver in the story is supposed to be compensated $200)

Driver's story #6: *"I've been an Uber driver for about six months. On my second day, a drunk girl pissed in the third row of my Highlander, soaking the carpet and leather seats, after she climbed over the second row, while the car was moving. She also exited completely bare-ass (and cooch) naked from the waist down. Her friends were so drunk that one literally fell out of the car and started crying when the boyfriend opened the door. It was a mess. She got banned and fined $200.*

I also have had to pull over for people to puke in the street, twice now, and last month I picked up a dealer from a strip club who passed out in my car and then left his bag. Finding that gallon sized bag of ganja was a spiritual experience for this broke college kid/pot head."

Driver's story #7: *"John. The dude who made me quit Uber three weeks into the experience. At 1 AM, I picked him up in a group of wasted college kids, didn't know they barely knew him. We got to our destination, everybody gets out, except John (that was his real name). I tapped to end the ride, only I realize everybody was leaving except this dude (I drove a minivan). I call everybody back to come and get their friend, but they had just partied together and knew nothing of him. We ask him where he lives, no answer. Blank look. I ask his friends to look for any ID. They found his driver's license in his pockets – turns out his name was John, and he lived two miles from there. I accepted to drive him for free (had ended my ride).*

He lived in this upper class neighborhood – million dollar houses left and right. At 2 AM, I got him in front of the address on his license. Except he could not walk and barely could stand up. I help him across the lawn to his front door, when he opens one eye and starts yelling in his drunk voice, "Who are you, and what are you doing on my father's property?" It is 2 AM, in the southern US, I am black, looking like I am wrestling this blond teenager. Did I mention it was around the time the US was embroiled in the Michael Brown saga? I left him there, crossed the lawn like Usain Bolt, got into my van, made a U-turn, and slammed away. The last thing I remember seeing/hearing is John shouting something, windows lighting up and dogs barking. I got home safely and never drove Uber again."

Driver's story #8: *"I did Uber and Lyft for awhile. I'll start by saying I'm in the minority as a female driver. I got hit on a lot because I was the last chance for drunk, male passengers to get laid. I really never encountered a terrible situation. I've overheard a lot of great conversations though. One time I was driving a group of Marines back to their base and they were telling me about this other Marine guy who had a fetish where he would stand on his head and jerk off into his own mouth."*

Driver's story #9: *"...So, at 11:05 last night, I made a pick up at a remote rural University of a visiting Japanese student. Her friend had booked a ride to take her home. She spoke almost no English and said that she had only been here two weeks. We are going along and it's a*

6 .4 mile trip. Suddenly at mile 6.0, just as I am about to make the turn to her street, the ride is cancelled. It's in an area with no streetlights. I ended up taking her almost to her destination for safety reasons. I can only assume the friend who ordered the ride watched on the app and saw she was almost home and wanted to avoid the fare. It initially showed up as cancelled and as a $3.19 fare. I contacted Uber support through the app and they have adjusted the ride for the full fare of $13.63."

Driver's story #10: (Moheeb): *"Guess what happened last weekend?? My wife and I went to eat at this nice restaurant in Hayes Valley S.F. and the waitress was this nice blonde. I happened to have given her an Uber ride to the mission a week before, after her shift ended.*

The bill was $64. I paid the $64 and gave no tip. The waitress approached me and asked if there was something wrong with the service?? I said no, and that the food was great. She said, 'You forgot to tip.'

I said, 'I left you the same tip you left me when I gave you an Uber ride home last weekend.' Her face was originally reddish, but it turned burgundy.. I enjoyed it very much!!!"

More stories at: www.facebook.com/groups/UberToronto

9.2 Riders' stories:

Rider's story #1: *"I caught an Uber to the airport two weeks ago and on the way there we got stuck in major traffic and I ended up missing my flight. Next one available was nine hours later so the Uber driver invited me back to his house and we chilled and played Mortal Kombat."*

Rider's story #2: *"I was smashed at a party and I called up an Uber. At the time I didn't realize it was my current high school history teacher... (cry and spooky icons) he now jokes about it in front of my class."*

Rider's story #3 (Jukie's Twitter): *"My Uber driver from earlier just texted me: Hey Julie, this is your Uber driver from tonight, Jeffrey! I just realized I forgot to give you a promo code [cutie for a free ride], but it's only valid if you use it on the way to dinner with me."*

Stories and comments of one star ratings:

Rider's comment #1: *"Stopped the car mid-trip to yell at a pigeon."* (rated:1 star)

Rider's comment #2: *"Radio was broken so he just kept making dubstep noises with his mouth the whole time."* (Rated: 1 star)

Driver's comment: *"No more candy, no more Aux core, no more gum, ...pax (passengers) garbage the bottle in my car. They don't deserve it."*

Driver's comment: *"Ever had to kick someone out of your vehicle? I just did.*

Guy started arguing with me over which way to get to his destination so I pulled over in a shopping mall, ended the ride (rated 1 star), told him his trip was over, and to exit my vehicle making sure he had anything that was his. HE REFUSED!!!! Nothing else I could do but call the police.

When they got there, I explained what happened. They asked him to get out and told me I was free to leave."

More stories: www.fb.com/groups/UberToronto

You might find that these stories and comments are funny and sarcastic. Indeed, there is something hidden in every story so as to help improve the Uber service experience with mutual respect from all participating parties: Uber, riders and drivers. Uber is committed to the best five star services. Uber also wants their customers and partners to be the finest Five Star individuals in the city.

Chapter 10: UBER & BUSINESS IDEAS

10.1 Uber affects business ideas:

This book has led you into the deepest insights of the biggest introduction of our era: UBER. UBER has numerous affects on business concepts. It reflects through Uber's current and new products and services such as UberEat, UberAccess, UberBike, UberRush, UberMOTO, ...and so on.

The smartness of the computering application is also affecting how young entrepreneurs think and do business. A few years after the Uber launch, many entrepreneurs have used UBER's business concept to implement their own new business ideas. In the United States of America, a group of entrepreneurs have launched their UberSex. In Toronto, a startup applied the Uber app idea for a massage and spa service. A lady has been working on something like "UberLaundry" with a combination of her name. We will see a lot more business ideas coming soon, based on the concept of the Uber app.

For the full list of businesses run based on Uber concept click here: fb.com/UberBook.KevinLy

10.2 Uber Toronto (Uber Canada) – Social Media Forum:

"Uber Toronto (All Partners)" (Official Forum Name as of September 23rd, 2016)
Link: www.fb.com/groups/UberToronto

Also known as:

- UberTO Driver Network
- Uber Ontario Driver Network
- Uber Canada Driver Network
- Uber Toronto Driver Network
- Uber Partners Coalition Association (Canadian Drivers)

'Uber Toronto (All Partners)" (www.fb.com/groups/UberToronto) is the most engaged communication forum for the Uber Toronto community. *Uber Toronto (All Partners)* board of members act like leaders for "Uber Partners Coalition Association" in Canada for Canadian drivers. *Uber Toronto (All Partners)* is also leading all other Uber Drivers foundations in more than 500 cities around the world. *Uber Toronto (All Partners)* is the first place to learn all the latest updates about the rideshare services. All Uber Driver Partners find it informative and supportive.

Uber Toronto (All Partners) official shopping store, called **Uber Partners Store** (www.UberPartnerStore.com), is the busiest Uber Online Shopping Center where thousands of Uber drivers are shopping 24/7 on a daily basis. They are periodically looking to purchase auto parts and other services from Canadian retailers and other businesses such as Canadian Tire, Autoshops, Auto Parts, GM, Dealers, etc. Are you a business owner? Does your store have something for Uber drivers? This all-in-one forum will absolutely boost your sales faster than any other client sources. To sell your products or services to Uber drivers, go here: www.UberPartnerStore.com or fb.com/groups/ UberToronto

Uber Toronto (All Partners): branded, real people, real target, real location, viewed multiple times, searched by media outlets, source of entrepreneurs in Toronto and other cities.

Before asking to join, you must read and respect our Terms and Agreements (Forum Policy):

Forum and Benefits:

- Uber Toronto (aka: Uber Canada): is the most engaged communication forum. All Uber Driver Partners find it informative, supportive and helpful.

- Uber Toronto includes all transportation platforms (UberX, UberXL, UberBlack, UberSelect, UberSUV, UberAccess, UberEat, UberDelivery, UberBike...)

- Mission: We listen to different sides to bring the most valuable service to our city (in terms of Employment Protection, Consumer Satisfaction, Business & Economy Growth, as well as Public Health & Safety)

Forum Policy:

1. Debate:
Respect one another. Keep it as the most neutral forum.

2. Content:
Discuss ONLY UBER or rideshare related topics.
- If you want to share a media post about Uber, please just take a screenshot with title and some main points (must hide the media company's name). Avoid free advertising (unintentionally) for media publishers and businesses.

3. Share (Sponsor):

All members are FREE to participate.

If you, however, wish to share a promotion, invitation, business link, or a sale, you are welcome to do so. Upon approval, you agree to sponsor for Ad Fee (check the current cost on: fb.com/groups/UberToronto) (unlimited on budget).

Why advertising on this Uber Toronto forum is better: branded, real people, real target, real location, viewed multiple times, searched by media outlets, source of entrepreneurs in Toronto and other cities.

4. Membership Benefits:

All members earn 10% commission by referring businesses into this group, upon a sale completion.

UBER Promotion Code: K94Y3

_ Drive: to start, you receive $100 from Uber to try driving for five days (Average: $1000 per week) by applying Uber Code: K94Y3)

_UberEat Promotion Code: Eats-K94Y3, redeem $10 off for your lunch and dinner.
*You must notify us at the time you sign up.

*the promotion is subject to change by time

5. Strict policy:

5a). (Read or Blocked)
Unauthorized posting or anything that violates Forum Terms and Agreements will be reminded and removed the first time; after that, the membership account will be permanently blocked.

5b). Post-blocked:
If you wish to have your name removed from the "blocked" list, and rejoin the forum in good standing, you then will have to agree to be charged $100.
After being blocked, you will NO longer have access into the forum; neither will you be able to find a contact. So, now, it is significant for you to keep in touch with admin team: LYSON MEDIA Team (fb.com/LysonMedia)

6. Board of Members:

We are calling high-profile members and leaders to join Uber Toronto Partner Association (backing drivers as a union) as:
One Public Speaker
One Secretary
Five Board members (on behalf of all partners)
*Submit your application to Kevin at www.facebook.com/KevinLy.Official
*For Public Speaker candidate: submit a short video in which you are

persuading how you are qualified for the position.

7. Contact:
Business inquiry: fb.com/LysonMedia
Forum Founder: Kevin Ly www.facebook.com/KevinLy.Official
Uber community: fb.com/UberToronto
Videos and Photos: fb.com/LysonMedia
UberBook: fb.com/UberBook.KevinLy
"Uber Toronto (All Partners)" (www.fb.com/groups/UberToronto)

10.3 About the Author:

Bio:

• Canadian Author, Entrepreneur, Brand Expert, and Philanthropist
(www.facebook.com/KevinLy.Offical)

• Founder and CEO at LYSON MEDIA Inc
(www.facebook.com/LysonMedia)

• Partners Ambassador and Founder of Uber Toronto (+All Partners)
forum (www.facebook.com/groups/UberToronto)
(www.UberPartnerStore.com)

• Executive Manager at American Facebookers forum
(www.facebook.com/groups/facbookers.LM)

- Author of "UBER – Good or Bad Economy"
(www.facebook.com/UberBook.KevinLy & www.BookOnUber.com)

- Business Partner with UBER and its CEO Travis Kalanick.
(www.facebook.com/UberToronto)

- Media Producer at Art Gallery World
(www.instagram.com/Art_Gallery_World)

- Personnel Manager at LM Models
(www.facebook.com/LysonMedia.Models)

10.4 About LYSON MEDIA Inc.:

LYSON MEDIA Inc. is the Leading Media Center for Entertainment, Technology, Business, and Living Knowledge.

Investment opportunities: LYSON MEDIA Inc. welcomes all investors for the next funding.

Watch our videos on www.facebook.com/LysonMedia

Website:
www.LysonMedia.ca
www.LysonMedia.com

Social Media: @LysonMedia
Email: info@LysonMedia.com

10.5 A message for young entrepreneurs:

This book is also written to encourage young entrepreneurs to start their business right away (as soon as possible), even if you are in the middle of making your decision for a perfect product or service. If you are stuck, in any way from knowing how to do it, then you had better start running now, and figure it out on the way. "Time and tide wait for no man." If you don't take action, your business idea will soon become someone else's profitable business. In fact, giant businesses like Facebook or Apple started their business from a very basic foundation. You don't want to look back at the first Facebook page because it is just a white landing page with a personal account login. Nobody wants to pay a penny for the first version of Apple's iphone. They all started simple and developed in the later stages into the current *perfection*. Before Uber was launched, no one knew how to bring private cars into a transportation service. They would be thinking of how much they would have to pay their drivers, and how could the rider trust the driver, etc. –and you are just stuck. You also know, Uber redesigned their logo after five successful years into the real business. The best recommendation is that your business idea should bring a vast value to people. If you are able to solve a real problem, you will succeed. Start now!

A Message from the Author

The numbers in this book, which are from media and research sources, might or might not be exact with the actual numbers, but it's precise enough to illustrate how strong your city's economy is by observing Uber platform differences and availability.

If your city already has Uber services that you really enjoy, just appreciate it.
If your city doesn't have Uber yet, just wait for it to be regulated. Or, talk to your city council to make the best service available in your city. Sooner or later, people have what they deserve to have.

If you find something that needs to be added, please do not hesitate to reach out to me: Kevin Lý (www.Facebook.com/KevinLy.Media)

My discussion and analysis is quite fair. *We listen to different sides to bring the most valuable services to our city in terms of Employment Protection, Consumer Satisfaction, Business & Economy Growth, as well as Public Health & Safety.*

Contact:

Forum Founder & Author:
Kevin Lý
Facebook: www.facebook.com/KevinLy.Official (preferred)
Email: Kevin.Ly@LysonMedia.com
Phone: 1 (416) 460 3523 (Toronto – Canada)

LYSON MEDIA inc:
Facebook: www.facebook.com/LysonMedia
Website: www.LysonMedia.com or www.LysonMedia.ca
Email: info@LysonMedia.com

Uber Toronto (All Partners): www.fb.com/groups/UberToronto
UBER community: fb.com/UberToronto
Videos and Photos: fb.com/LysonMedia
Book: fb.com/UberBook.KevinLy or www.BookonUBER.com
UBER Partners Store: www.UberPartnerStore.com

Important: Uber Technologies Inc keeps updating their app and policies from time to time. By the time, you got this book in hand, there may be newer information. The author and his team will follow up the changes and keep the content up-to-date in the next editions of the book. Or you can check it on the following websites for prompt updates:

fb.com/UberBook.KevinLy
fb.com/groups/UberToronto
www.BookOnUber.com

www.ingramcontent.com/pod-product-compliance
Lightning Source LLC
Chambersburg PA
CBHW031121210326
41519CB00047B/4229